The
Catholic Marriage
Wisdom Book

Donna Marie Cedar-Southworth

Our Sunday Visitor Publishing Division
Our Sunday Visitor, Inc.
Huntington, Indiana 46750

Scripture citations used in this work are taken from various translations and are cited throughout. The author and publisher are grateful to all copyright holders whose material appears in the text and who are acknowledged in the "Notes" section at the end of the book. If any copyrighted material has been inadvertently used without proper credit being given in one manner or another, please notify Our Sunday Visitor so future printings of this work may be corrected.

Our Sunday Visitor Publishing Division
Our Sunday Visitor, Inc.
200 Noll Plaza
Huntington, IN 46570

ISBN: 087973-410-8
LCCCN: 00-130463

Edited by Lisa Grote
Cover design by Monica Haneline
PRINTED IN THE UNITED STATES OF AMERICA

ACKNOWLEDGMENTS

A sincere thanks to all of the couples who participated in my study by sharing their most intimate thoughts on marriage with me. Thank you for encouraging me to pass on your thoughts and reflections by referring to you as "anonymous," throughout the book, but allowing me to acknowledge you by name in this section. I sincerely thank:

Father Daniel S. Spychala, Polly and John Cedar, Fred and Mary Doyle, Bernice and Ted Krivoruchka, Jack and Sheila Leonard, Helen and Jack Meagher, E. Dornell and Vice Admiral Kilcline, Dottie Keene, Betty and Norm Violette, Dottie and George Washko, Terry Baskerville, Carol and Joe Kuhn, Mary Francis and Hank Kinney, Dr. and Mrs. Charles Schehl, Mary Eversoll, Dolores Leckey, Sandy and Will Sardelli, Dr. and Mrs. George Fleury, Marie Kordes, Dr. and Mrs. Evers, Betty and Sam Bridgeman, Freddie Wall, Emily and Edward Shaunessy, Loretta and Bill Delaney, Marjorie Holmes, Midge and Joe Wholey, Gilbert and Donja Donahue, Mike and Genevieve Timpane, Sally and Al Galiani, Brinton and Phillis Brown, Helen and Martin McCavitt, Mr. and Mrs. Mancuso, Elise and Carl Siebentritt, Kathy and Bill Standiford, Judy and Fred Degnan, Barbara Murphy-Edwards, Joan Urbanczyk, Betty and Bill Reckmeyer, Marie and Dick Chomeau, John and Barbara Ahearne, Mary Ellen Cannon, The Jelinecks, Mr. and Mrs. Brown, The Chalmers, The McCaffreys, The Welchs, Catherine Jones, all the wonderful and loving residents at Falcon's Landing who shared their intimate stories with me; my best friend Theresa, who gave me the idea for this book; and my beloved daughter Gabriella and my loving husband Scott.

CONTENTS

INTRODUCTION

This book started out as a compilation of stories told to me in personal interviews by couples who had been married fifty years or so. I wanted to know how Catholicism and their faith in God had solidified their marriages over the years. My hope was that I could pass on the secrets of people who had chosen to weather the storm, no matter how difficult. Not surprisingly, these charming senior citizens wanted to remain anonymous, so as not to appear as though they were pontificating or claiming to have all "the answers," though clearly they have some unique and seasoned insight worth passing on to generations to come.

The book evolved into a series of thirteen chapters, which include some personal stories and recommendations these couples shared with me in personal interviews; it includes mainly, however, Church teachings, theology, Scripture, and excerpts from a great number of sources on spirituality in marriage. Each chapter dictated to me its own distinct personality that seemed to grow out of necessity to address that particular subject matter most appropriately.

Where you see an "anonymous" attributed to a source, know that it is a person talking directly to you, imparting some words of wisdom as eloquently as they know how. They remain in the background but will live forever in the pages of this book and are gratefully cited in the acknowledgments.

It is my hope that the content of this book, particular passages and personal stories herein, will resonate with you as they have with me. And I hope that it will help you — in the best and in the worst of times — to weather the storms of life and to find comfort and solace in the Lord and His teachings. Above all, I hope this book will enrich your understanding of the Sacrament of Matrimony as it has, indeed, mine.

The Sacrament of Matrimony can be
compared to the "Sanctuary"
because it must include not only the union
of husband and wife,
but Jesus Christ as well . . . all three
united together.
Jesus is always present in the
Sanctuary of the Church,
and that's why
it's an apt comparison:
because He is ALWAYS present in marriage.

Even if husband and wife choose
to separate themselves,
or walk away from the Sanctuary of Marriage,
Christ's Body and Presence remains there . . .
waiting for their return.

— Father Daniel S. Spychala,
personal interview, April 30, 1999

Chapter 1.

THE PURPOSE OF MARRIAGE

Marriage has God for its Author, and was from the very beginning a kind of foreshadowing of the incarnation of His Son; and therefore there abides in it a something holy and religious; not extraneous, but innate; not derived from men, but implanted by nature.

— Pope Leo XIII,
Arcanum Divinae Sapientia,
February 10, 1880

Since every man is a part of the human race, and human nature is something social and possesses the capacity for friendship as a great and natural good, for this reason God wished to create all men from one, so that they might be held together in their society, not only by the similarity of race, but also by the bond of blood relationship. And so it is that the first natural tie of human society is man and wife.

— St. Augustine,
The Good Marriage, 1 (5th century)

It is a fusion of two hearts — the union of two lives — the coming together of two tributaries, which, after being joined in marriage, will flow in the same channel in the same direction . . . carrying the same burdens of responsibility and obligation.

— Peter Marshall, in Catherine Marshall's
A Man Called Peter

And the Lord God said, "It isn't good for man to be alone; I will make a companion for him, a helper suited to his needs." So the Lord God formed from the soil every kind of animal and bird, and brought them to the man to see what he would call them; and whatever he called them, that was their name. But still there was no proper helper for the man. Then the Lord God caused the man to fall into a deep sleep, and took one of his ribs and closed up the place from which he had removed it, and made the rib into a woman, and brought her to the man.

"This is it!" Adam exclaimed. "She is part of my own bone and flesh! Her name is woman because she was taken out of a man." This explains why a man leaves his father and mother and is joined to his wife in such a way that the two become one person.

— Genesis 2:18-25,
The Way, Complete Catholic Edition Bible

The goal in marriage is not to think alike, but to think together.
— Robert C. Dodds, *Two Together*

How shall we ever be able to adequately describe the happiness of that marriage which the Church arranges, the Sacrifice strengthens, upon which the blessing sets a seal, at which the angels are present as witnesses, and to which the Father gives His consent.
— Tertullian, *To His Wife* (3rd century)

And such a bliss is there betwixt them two
That save the joy that lasteth evermo,
There is none like, that any creature
Hath seen or shall, while that the
world may dure.
— William Chaucer,
Tale of the Man of Lawe (14th century)

Where the flesh is one, one also is the spirit. Together husband and wife pray, together perform their fasts, mutually teaching, exhorting, sustaining. Equally they are found in the church of God, equally at the banquet of God, equally in persecutions and in refreshments.
— Tertullian, *To His Wife* (3rd century)

Marriage, before being a union of bodies, is first and more intimately a union and harmony of minds, brought about not by any passing affection of sense or heart but by a deliberate and resolute decision of the will; and from this cementing of minds, by God's decree, there arises a sacred and inviolable bond.

— Pope Pius XI, *Casti Connubi,*
December 31, 1930

Female and male God made the man,
His image is the whole, not half.

— Coventry Patmore,
The Angel in the House (19th century)

As a Sacrament, marriage gives people the supernatural strength necessary to "fight the good fight." Every victory achieved together over habit, routine, and boredom cements the bonds existing between the spouses and makes their love produce new blossoms.

— Dietrich Von Hildebrand,
Marriage: The Mystery of Faithful Love

And when will there be an end of marrying? I suppose, when there is an end of living!

— Tertullian, *An Exhortation to Chastity*, 10
(3rd century)

Marriage is a sacred vocation. As a married man or woman, you have one of the greatest gifts — and one of the greatest opportunities to do good — that is possible for human beings to possess on earth. In your sacrament of marriage, you have a vocation from God — a special call by Him to you and your mate — to serve Him together in a holy sacrament until death.

— Reverend George Anthony Kelly,
The Catholic Marriage Manual

That there is something intrinsically sacred in the marriage contract is evidenced by the fact that all religions, even the most corrupt, always have regarded it as such and surrounded it with religious rites and ceremonies.

— K.J.I. Hochban, *Canadian Messenger of the Sacred Heart*, August, 1950

Mysterious is the fusion of two loving spirits: each takes the best from the other, but only to give it back again enriched with love.

— Romain Rolland, *Jean Christopher*

Conjugal love involves a totality, in which *all* the elements of the person enter — appeal of the body and instinct, power of feeling and affectivity, aspiration of the spirit and of will. It aims at a deeply personal unity, a unity that, beyond union in one flesh, leads to forming one heart and soul. . . . In a word, it is a question of the normal characteristics of all natural conjugal love, but with a new significance which not only purifies and strengthens them but raises them to the extent of making them the expression of specifically Christian values.

— *Familiaris Consortio* in
Catechism of the Catholic Church, 1643

Becoming aware of yourselves as spiritual beings transforms your marriage into a sacred place.

— Evelyn and Paul Moschetta,
The Marriage Spirit

It takes three to make Love in Heaven —
Father, Son, and Holy Spirit.

It takes three for Heaven to make love to
earth —
God, Man, and Mary, through whom God
became Man.

It takes three to make love in the Holy family —
Mary, and Joseph, and the consummation of
their love, Jesus.

It takes three to make love in hearts —
The Lover, the Beloved, and Love.
— Bishop Fulton Sheen,
Three to Get Married

Marriage is a triangular relationship . . .
with Jesus as the head.
— Sam and Betty Bridgeman,
personal interview

You must recognize that your marriage is something greater than even both of you put together. It is possible for you to have an ideal marriage even though husband and wife are but ordinary people. Each of you may acquire qualities that were not found in either prior to marriage, and both come to the pleasant realization that the whole is *greater* than the sum of its parts.

— Reverend George E. Kelly,
The Catholic Marriage Manual

Marriage is an act that signifies and involves a mutual gift, which unites the spouses and binds them to their eventual souls, with whom they make up a sole family — a domestic church.

— John Paul II, quoted in
the London *Observer*, January 31, 1982

Adam could not be happy even in Paradise without Eve.

— John Lubbock, *Peace and Happiness*

Christian marriage, like the other sacraments, "whose purpose is to sanctify people, to build up the body of Christ, and finally, to give worship to God," is in itself a liturgical action glorifying God in Jesus Christ and in the church. By celebrating it, Christian spouses profess their gratitude to God for the sublime gift bestowed on them of being able to live their married and family lives the very love of God for people and that of the Lord Jesus for the church, His bride.

— John Paul II, *Familiaris Consortio,*
December 15, 1981

The sacrament of Matrimony signifies the union of Christ and the Church. It gives spouses the grace to love each other with the love with which Christ has loved his Church; the grace of the sacrament thus perfects the human love of the spouses, strengthens their indissoluble unity, and sanctifies them on the way to eternal life.

— Council of Trent: DS 1799,
Catechism of the Catholic Church, 1661

From the first, a Christian marriage is intentionally more than just the communion for the whole of life of this man and this woman. It is more than just human covenant; it is also religious covenant. It is more than law and obligations and rights; it is also grace. From the first, God and God's Christ are present as third partners in it, modeling it, gracing it, and guaranteeing. The presence of grace in its most ancient and solemn Christian sense, namely the presence of the gracious God, is not something extrinsic to Christian marriage. It is something *essential* to it.

— Michael Lawler,
Marriage and Sacrament

A person truly in love wants to bind himself forever to his beloved — which is precisely the gift that marriage gives him.

— Dietrich Von Hildebrand,
Marriage: the Mystery of Faithful Love

The crucifix is a classroom where a couple can learn about love because Christ's love for us on the cross shows us the unconditional, freewill love for us . . . and *that's* the same love that husband and wife must have for one another.

— Father Daniel S. Spychala,
personal interview

To wed is to bring not only our worldly goods but every potential capacity to create more values in living together. . . . In becoming one these two create a new world that had never existed before.

— Paul E. Johnson, *Christian Love*

Chapter 2.

THE FIRST YEAR

The wedding ring, symbolical of the conjugal relation, has ever been the accepted accompaniment of marriage. Its being put on the fourth finger of the left hand has been continued, from long-established usage, because of the fanciful conceit that from this finger a nerve went direct to the heart.

— Frederick Saunders,
Salad for the Solitary and the Social, 1871

No great thing is created suddenly
any more than a bunch of grapes or a fig.
If you tell me that you desire a fig,
I answer that there must be time.
Let it first blossom,
then bear fruit,
then ripen.

— Epictetus, *Discourses*

The realities of a marriage often turn out to be quite different from the expectations. When two people marry, they are novices in the ways of love. So they fill the vacuum of their ignorance with pleasant anticipations. The marriage they look forward to will never be costly, often ecstatic, and always delightful. Then slowly, inexorably their life together replaces their illusions with the actualities, their fantasies with the facts. When their anticipations and their experiences don't match up, they are surprised. . . . But the real shock comes when one experiences the truth of Dostoevski's monk Zosima's saying: "A true act of love, unlike imaginary love, is hard and forbidding." Our love must be ingrained in the textures of our everyday life together. . . . Rarely do we envision the demands of love we shall have to give, the struggles we shall have to go through to be and do all that it requires of us. . . . Yet, to know what love really is and to enjoy what it holds in store for us, we find we must give as well as receive. For giving and receiving interfuse in married love.

— Jon Nilson, *From This Day Forward*

You have to have a deep love and respect for each other. And just as important is the love you have for the Lord and all of His teachings. It is important to communicate with each other about *all* things— both small and large — until you have reached a mutual agreement. This creates for open communication and for a happy atmosphere in your home. We have found a successful relationship often involves putting your spouse's needs ahead of your own.

— Anonymous (Married fifty-one years;
two children; three grandchildren)

In real love you want the other person's good.
In romantic love you want the other person.

— Margaret Anderson, *A Woman's Note Book*

Both artist and lover know that perfection is
not lovable.
It is the clumsiness of a fault that makes a
person lovable.

— Joseph Campbell,
as cited in *Running on Empty*

Twelve Rules for a Happy Marriage

1. Never both be angry at once.
2. Never yell at each other unless the house is on fire.
3. Yield to the wishes of the other as an exercise in self-discipline, if you can't think of a better reason.
4. If you have a choice between making yourself or your mate look good — choose your mate.
5. If you feel you must criticize, do so lovingly.
6. Never bring up a mistake of the past.
7. Neglect the whole world rather than each other.
8. Never let the day end without saying at least one complimentary thing to your life partner.
9. Never meet without an affectionate greeting.
10. When you've made a mistake, talk it out and ask for forgiveness.
11. Remember it takes two to make an argument. The one who is wrong is the one who will be doing most of the talking.
12. Never go to bed mad.

—Unknown

In authentic love, the other is accepted not as a god but as a gift of God. As a gift of God, the other is unique and irreplaceable, a sacred trust, a mission to be fulfilled. As Dante said, speaking of Beatrice: "She looks on Heaven, and I look on her." There are perhaps few more touchingly beautiful spectacles in all the world than that of a husband and wife saying their prayers together. The prayer of a husband and wife, said together, is not the same as two distinct individuals pouring out their hearts to God, for in the first instance there is an acknowledgment of the Spirit of Love, which makes them one. Because both are destined for eternity, it is fitting that all their acts of love have that eternal flavor in which their souls in prayer and their bodies in marriage attest to the universality of admiration not only for God but also for each other.

— Bishop Fulton Sheen,
Three to Get Married

The course of true love never did run smooth.

— William Shakespeare,
A Midsummer Night's Dream
Act 1, Scene 1

We found it is important to allow each other room to differ. And sometimes we differ very strongly, but we are able to reconcile that and to accept our differences — to let it be O.K. that he's not like me, and I'm not just like him. You don't have to think and feel the same way all the time . . . and along with that goes "patience." You really have to be patient with that whole idea and work at it.

— Anonymous (Married forty-one years;
six children, four grandchildren)

Sacred union of souls beneath the immortal yoke of love freely promised, pleasures and duties for ever in common, misfortunes borne together, joys of paternity tempered by the anxieties of the future, indescribably mingling of good and evil, virtue ever present to sustain the feebleness of the heart against the chafings and trials of life.

— Jean Baptiste Lacordaire (1802-61), *Thoughts and Teachings of Jean Baptiste Lacordaire*

Take care of the minutes,
for the hours will take care of themselves.

— Lord Chesterfield

When two people marry, chances are they are not at the same psychological and geographical distances from their respective families. When my wife Diane and I married in Chicago, we were both relatively equidistant from our families psychologically: we had each achieved about the same emotional independence from our parents. But geographically? That was another story. My parents lived in Pittsburgh. Diane's lived only two blocks away! For the first two years of our marriage we were within shouting distance of them. Fortunately, neither of us came from a family of shouters! In fact, Diane's mother was so sensitive to the situation that when she saw us walking down the street, she would cross over to the other side and pretend she had not seen us coming. How wonderful if everyone's mother-in-law were so considerate! Of course we told her that she did not have to avoid us for fear of interfering with our new marriage.

In a sense, every newly married couple has to discover ways to get the mother-in-law and the father-in-law, the brothers and sisters, and even old friends to cross to the other side of the street. Why? Because new boundaries need to be drawn between the newlyweds and the people who had previously played such important roles in their lives. The old attachments to parents, friends, and siblings need to be redefined so that the married couple can establish a family space that is uniquely and privately their own. They must learn to live in their own way with as little unwanted intrusion from outsiders as possible.

— Harvey L. Ruben, M.D., *Supermarriage*

I think it's very important in a marital relationship to have a light touch, and sometimes say to oneself, "What's this or that really going to matter in 100 years?" You have to have a sense of humor and sometimes a light, very light touch.

— Anonymous (Married forty-two years;
five children; three grandchildren)

Ah, love let us be true
To one another! For the world, which seems
To lie before us like a land of dreams,
So various, so beautiful, so new,
Hath really neither joy, nor love, nor light,
Nor certitude, nor peace, nor help for pain;
And we are here as on a darkling plain
Swept with confused alarms of struggle
and flight,
Where ignorant armies clash by night.

— Matthew Arnold, *Dover Beach*

In the book of Deuteronomy, it is prescribed:

> "When a man is newly married, he shall not be liable for military service or any other public duty. He shall remain at home exempt from service for one year and enjoy the wife he has taken" (24:5).

The *New American Bible's* translation sounds a slightly different note from the new English Bible's above:

> "When a man is newly wed, he need not go out on a military expedition, nor shall any public duty be imposed on him. He shall be exempt for one year for the sake of his family, to bring joy to the wife he has married."

It is fascinating to note that even the claims of public need and national necessity are put below the wants of the newly married spouses.

— Jon Nilson, *From This Day Forward*

One of the most important things is that you need to allow each other to grow. When you're first married, sometimes you expect that your partner is going to fulfill everything for you, and I think that's a mistake. I think you have to realize that you are both going to develop, probably at different speeds, and you've got a lot more growing to do. You really have to allow and support each one in developing their own talents. At times they will blossom and you will coast, but then, probably at a different time, you will blossom, and then they will coast and support you in your efforts.

— Anonymous (Married fifty-one years;
seven children; fifteen grandchildren)

Remember, a happy marriage is not one that has no problems, but one that can solve problems.

— Martin G. Olsen, Ed. D. and
George Von Kaenel, S.J., *Two as One*

We seek in "another" what God alone can give us, and to many this search has seemed mad; on the one hand to those who do not know what love is and see in it only the need and the cry of the flesh, but on the other hand to those also who have built between the love of God and the love of creatures the impassable barrier of Manichaeism [heresy] or, worse still, of Jansenism [condemned as heretical by papal authority].

But in truth for those who are not called to the high vocation of loving God alone, the way to the love of God is still to be found through the love of creatures.

. . . We need to be more than ourselves, to enter into the great gesture of Creation which is inseparably both gift and love. Another being brings to us this extension of existence in the union of love. But how can there be union without common life? It is in this context that the words of Scripture take on their full meaning: they shall be *one flesh*. And not only in the flesh but in all their human being.

. . . We need this other being. Not just any other, but this particular other . . . *We take* this other one. So the need for permanence in marriage is rooted in the very heart of human nature.

— Jean De Fabregues, *Christian Marriage*

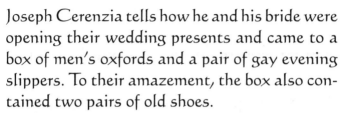

Joseph Cerenzia tells how he and his bride were opening their wedding presents and came to a box of men's oxfords and a pair of gay evening slippers. To their amazement, the box also contained two pairs of old shoes.

"Why those are my old shoes!" exclaimed the bride.

"And mine, too," said the groom. He opened the enclosed envelope and took out a twenty dollar bill and letter:

Dear Son:
These new shoes I give you and your wife
to tread your way along
the path of married life.
In the beginning marriage, like these shoes,
can be a tight fit and may pinch.
But as the days, weeks, and years pass,
you will find that your marriage
grows more satisfying, more perfect —
And as comfortable as the worn old shoes.
I wish you both a pleasant journey.
Your loving father.
— Father John A. O'Brien, Ph.D., LL.D.,
Happy Marriage

Chapter 3.

WHEN THE SPARKS STOP FLYING

The greatest illusion of lovers is to believe that the intensity of their sexual attraction is the guarantee of the perpetuity of their love. It is because of this failure to distinguish between the glandular and the spiritual . . . that marriages are so full of deception.

— Bishop Fulton J. Sheen,
Three to Get Married

Sex is just one of 100 ways to say, "I love you." If relied on too much or if it is the only way of saying "I love you," it becomes an empty sign (symbol). It becomes just an excuse for pleasure rather than an act which really sums up all the love given that day or week. The best act of sex is that which begins in the morning at the breakfast table with the kindness shown there and continued all day with consideration and small acts of affection.

— Martin Olsen, Ed.D. and
George Von Kaenel, S.J., *Two as One*

Such love, merging the human with divine, leads the spouses to a free and mutual gift of themselves, a gift proving itself by gentle affection and deed. . . . It far excels mere erotic inclination, which selfishly pursued, soon enough fades away.

— Walter M. Abbott, S.J., *The Church Today*

. . . Once married, you each will have a right to normal marital relations. The law of the Church for ages has spelled this out: each spouse has a right to those acts which of their nature are ordered toward the procreation of children. This means that you will also have a corresponding duty not to refuse the reasonable request of your spouse for honest marital relations. (Do not use sex as a weapon.) It means further that each of you has the duty of making such activity true acts of marital love, acts which can honestly symbolize the self-giving and caring love you pledge when you marry.

— John F. Kippley, *Marriage Is for Keeps*

The first communion is the one which is established and which develops between husband and wife: By virtue of the covenant of married life, the man and woman "are no longer two but one flesh" and they are called to grow continually in their communion through day-to-day fidelity to their marriage promise of total mutual self-giving.

— Pope John Paul II, *Familiaris Consortio*,
December 15, 1981

Fidelity to small things will lead you to Christ. Infidelity to small things will lead you to sin.

— Mother Teresa, *The Love of Christ*

It takes three to make love. What binds lover and beloved together on earth is an ideal outside both. As it is impossible to have rain without clouds, so it is impossible to understand love without God.

— Bishop Fulton Sheen,
Three to Get Married

THE GOLDEN RULE

From the time I was a little girl, my mother and father taught me, "first comes respect, then comes love." Ours was a home environment where this philosophy was the golden rule. For this child to understand and feel the importance of respect, came the reward of unconditional love.

Falling "in love" later in life is another story. Initially, the experience runs the gamut of emotions. Many of us will remember our hearts throbbing, our senses blurred, our temperatures rising! It is a breathtakingly exquisite sensation. Eventually, after a few years of marriage and children, when the pulse returns to normal, and the real world of everyday problems and challenges emerges, our hearts settle down to a steady beat and our head clears.

Where are we? Have we chosen the kind of partner with whom we really look forward to spending the rest of our lives? Have we created a bond within our marriage based on fidelity, friendship and forgiveness? If the answer is "yes," we have also achieved the kind of love and commitment born of respect — one for the other — destined to survive the uncharted waters ahead

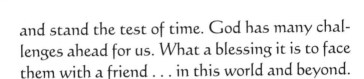

and stand the test of time. God has many challenges ahead for us. What a blessing it is to face them with a friend . . . in this world and beyond.

— Anonymous

The physical union of husband and wife constitutes such an ultimate intimacy between them that of its essence it is a surrender valid once and for all. It is not merely a passing intimacy which establishes no objective relationship. It implies a definite decision of the highest import. It is truly a *surrender* of one's self to the other and implies essentially the same exclusiveness which we found in conjugal love.

— Dietrich Von Hildebrand,
Marriage: the Mystery of Faithful Love

Touch is one of the most expressive forms of human communication.

— John L. Thomas, S.J.,
Beginning Your Marriage

Because our laziness, our dullness, and our constant falling back into the periphery stultifies our vision, it is difficult always to keep before us in all its same clarity and splendor the image of the other person so wonderfully revealed by love. We should and must fight against this dullness, for it constitutes a sin against the temple which we erected in our marriage.

— Dietrich Von Hildebrand,
Marriage: The Mystery of Faithful Love

The second hardest thing in all the world is to engage in the trying process of living intimately with one other person. The hardest thing in all the world is living alone.

— John L. Thomas, S.J.,
Beginning Your Marriage

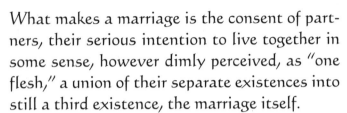

What makes a marriage is the consent of partners, their serious intention to live together in some sense, however dimly perceived, as "one flesh," a union of their separate existences into still a third existence, the marriage itself.

— William G. Cole,
Sex in Christianity and Psychoanalysis

. . . as time goes on, the experience [sex], loses its novelty and its urgency. Like starving refugees who come to the land of plenty, at first they gorge themselves on the experience as if there were no tomorrow. Then slowly they come to realize that there is a tomorrow and a tomorrow after that and a multitude of tomorrows. What was unexplored becomes familiar. What was experiment becomes routine. And what was spark seems to become ashes.

. . . But there are still possibilities to be discovered, areas to be explored — not in the sexual act itself but in each other. . . . From now on, what will make the sexual relationship new and fascinating are not just the actions the couple performs but the *persons they are*.

— Jon Nilson, *From This Day Forward*

Of all the misconceptions about love, the most powerful and pervasive is the belief that "falling in love" is love or at least one of the manifestations of love . . . but two problems are immediately apparent. The first is that the experience of falling in love is specifically a sex-linked erotic experience. We do not fall in love with our children even though we may love them very deeply. We do not fall in love with our friends . . . we fall in love only when we are consciously or unconsciously sexually motivated. The second problem is that the experience of falling in love is invariably temporary. No matter whom we fall in love with, we sooner or later fall out of love if the relationship continues long enough. This is not to say that we invariably cease loving the person with whom we fell in love. But it is to say that the feeling of ecstatic lovingness that characterizes the experience of falling in love always passes. The honeymoon always ends. The bloom of romance always fades.

. . . To the contrary, real love often occurs in a context in which the feeling of love is lacking, when we act lovingly despite the fact that we don't feel loving.

— M. Scott Peck, M.D.,
The Road Less Traveled

Don't for one moment imagine that marriage is going to be one long, romantic honeymoon. Don't overstress what is physical, for you will find that but a small part of happiness in marriage is dependent upon the senses. The physical attraction will diminish and give place to a greater and nobler basis for happiness. Don't forget that, although you may find it hard to realize, your love will lose its ardor and so will your fiancé's. If you nourish it, it will develop in its maturity into something deep and glorious; but it will lose its glamour and you won't find it as simple as you do now to be on the alert to please him, and neither will he be able to make sacrifices for you without effort.

— Father A.H. Dolan, O.Carm., *Happy Marriage*

We are not born lovers.
Love is a task,
a skill,
an art
we must work at
until the day we die!

— John L. Thomas, S.J.,
Beginning Your Marriage

Chapter 4.

WALKING THE JOURNEY TOGETHER

Come, live with me and be my love,
And we will all the pleasures prove
Of peace and plenty, bed and board,
That chance employment may afford.

I'll handle the dainties on the docks
And thou shalt read of summer frocks:
At evening by the sour canals
We'll hope to hear some madrigals.

Care on thy maiden brow shall put
A wreath of wrinkles, and thy foot
Be shod with pain: not silken dress
But toil shall tire thy loveliness.

Hunger shall make thy modest zone
And cheat fond death of all but bone —
If these delights thy mind may move,
Then live with me and be my love.

> — Christopher Marlowe,
> *The Passionate Shepherd to His Love*

The sacrament of Matrimony has this specific
element that distinguishes it from all the
other sacraments:
it is the sacrament of something that was
part of the very economy of creation;
it is the very conjugal covenant instituted
by the Creator "in the beginning."
Therefore, the decision of a man and a
woman to marry
in accordance with this divine plan, that is to say,
the decision to commit by their irrevocable
conjugal consent their whole lives
in indissoluble love and unconditional fidelity,
really involves, even if not in a fully conscious way,
an attitude of profound obedience
to the will of God,
an attitude which cannot exist
without God's grace.
They have thus already begun what is in a
true and proper sense
a journey towards salvation,
a journey which the celebration of the
sacrament and the immediate preparation for it
can complement and bring to completion,
given the uprightness of their intention.
— Pope John Paul II, *Familiaris Consortio*

. . . go on, and I will follow thee,
To the last gasp,
with truth
and loyalty.
— William Shakespeare, *As You Like It*

A successful marriage is an edifice that must be rebuilt every day.
— André Maurois, *The Art of Living*,
"The Art of Marriage"

Love and marriage are a lot like a flower garden. It is never enough to plant the seeds and then to sit back and wait for the flowers to grow. The seeds must be lovingly watered and fed, the garden must be assiduously weeded if the garden is to grow. So it is with love and marriage. If they are to grow into a thing of beauty, they must be watered and nurtured and weeded by lovers and spouses.

— Michael G. Lawler,
Marriage and Sacrament

We must take up our life as our life is today. We must commit to the bodies we have, to the children we have, to where we live and work, even to the physical symptoms we have this instant and to whatever mess we have caused that we find ourselves in today. In other words, we commit to mistakes as well as to the mistakes of others. We see clearly and recognize them as part of our path home — even as we take steps to stop making the mistakes.

No matter what the picture of our life, we must turn to God anyway. In every small encounter, in every detail of every circumstance, we must turn to God. And we must keep doing this until each activity becomes a prayer. Cleaning up the dog hair, balancing the checkbook, waiting for someone who is late, firing an employee, saying yes, saying no — whatever we find before us is nothing more than an opportunity to know the peace of God. Not a code of conduct, it does not look a certain way — it feels a certain way.

— Hugh Prather, *For the Love of God,*
"Walking Home"

. . . We love because we are not sufficient
to ourselves.
The man who turns in upon himself
and lives for himself alone
does not love and is not loved.
The true mystery of love lies in this,
that in the leaving of self,
to which act love impels us,
we take in giving
and are taken by our gift.
We love because we are not sufficient
to ourselves . . .
— Jean De Fabregues, *Christian Marriage*

Chains do not hold a marriage together. It is
threads, hundreds of tiny threads which sew
people together through the years. That is what
makes a marriage last — more than passion or
even sex.

— Simone Signoret, London,
Daily Mail, July 4, 1978

In marriage you are neither the husband nor the
wife; you are the love between the two.

— Nisargadatta

Let us have *love* and more love; a love that melts all opposition, a love that conquers all foes, a love that sweeps away all barriers, a love that aboundeth in charity, a large-heartedness, tolerance, forgiveness and noble striving, a love that triumphs over all obstacles.

— Abdul Baha, *I Heard Him Say*

Marriage is that relation between man and woman in which the independence is equal, the dependence mutual, and the obligation reciprocal.

— Louis K. Anspacher, *Address,*
December 30, 1934

When you have reached a point where you no longer expect a response, you will at last be able to give your love in such a way that the other is able to receive and be grateful.

— Dag Hammarskjold, *Markings*

A happy marriage perhaps represents the ideal of human relationship — a setting in which each partner, while acknowledging the need of the other, feels free to be what he or she by nature is: a relationship in which instinct as well as intellect can find expression; in which giving and taking are equal; in which each accepts the other, and I confronts Thou.

— Anthony Storr,
The Integrity of the Personality

Marriage is a life where each asks from each what each most wants to give — and each awakes in each what else would never be.

— Edwin Muir, *Partners in Love*

Marriage and faith are like peeling an onion . . .
they both go through many stages
and mean different things
at different times.

— Dolores R. Leckey, personal inteview

The sheltered lives we lead encourage us to become thoughtless. We are encouraged to flit from moment to moment, activity to activity, possession to possession, person to person. The beauty to be found only through commitment is thus inaccessible to us. In fact, we are increasingly told today that commitment is not beautiful. It is said, for example, that lifelong commitment in marriage is an arbitrary holdover from a bygone religious age. Actually, whatever marriage may be, it is not arbitrary. Its foundations are in the depths of our own person; it is in that deep longing genuinely to know another person and truly to be known ourselves. To hedge on our commitment to another is really to hedge on how much we think they are worth. It takes time to discover worth. Its full depths are not apparent from the start. We have to venture, to act with faith that there is more than we have seen so far. A genuine marriage is a pledge of faith that we love enough to go into the future, with the confidence that another person is worthy of our lifelong devotion. It is also the humble reception of another person's faith in our being worthy of his or her lifelong devotion.

— Dr. Diogenese Allen, *Temptations*

People who have been married for many years sometimes speak of the depth of intimacy felt by being quiet together, simply being in the same room or the same house, conscious of each other's presence. There may be little or no conversation or direct interaction of any kind, but there is a feeling of nearness that comes from a reservoir of shared experience. It builds up bit by bit over the years to an intense awareness of the other.

Persons of prayer will recognize similarities in the cycles of marital intimacy and the cycles of the spiritual life. Periods of dryness in prayer, indifference, fatigue, inner turmoil, as well as delight and consolation are well-known on the spiritual journey. Through experience and reflection, though, we come to know God in the periods of absence as well as presence. In marriage, as in prayer, sometimes the appropriate response is simply to wait.

— Dolores R. Leckey, *The Ordinary Way*

A life allied with mine, for the rest of our lives — that is the miracle of marriage.

— Denis De Rougemont

. . be thou faithful until death,
and I will give thee a crown of life.
— The Revelation of St. John the Divine, 2:10,
King James Version Bible

Love never grows old except to those who put its essence into that which grows old: the body. Like a precious liquid, love shares the lot of the container. If love is put in a vessel of clay, it is quickly absorbed and dried; if, like knowledge, it is placed in the mind, it grows through the years, becoming stronger, even as the body grows weaker. The more it is united with the spirit, the more immortal it becomes. Just as some theologians know about God in an abstract way, so there are some who love only from afar. As other theologians know God through abandonment to His Will, so there are those who know love because they sought it in God's way and not their own. Once the spirit of Divine Love enters marriage, as it does at the altar, there is no magic faith introduced that the partner is absolutely perfect. But there is introduced the idea that this partner has been given by God until death and, therefore, is worthy of love for Christ's sake, always.

— Bishop Fulton Sheen, *Three to Get Married*

The form of matrimony consists in an inseparable union of minds; a couple are pledged to one
another in faithful friendship. The end is the be-
getting and upbringing of children, through marriage intercourse and shared duties in which
each helps the other to rear children.

— St. Thomas Aquinas,
Summa Theologica (13th century)

Love seeketh not itself to please,
Nor for itself hath any care,
But for another gives its ease,
And builds a heaven in Hell's despair.

— William Blake,
The Clod and the Pebble

Home of wildest hope and deepest despair, of the most unbridled selfishness and sometimes the most absolute renunciation, of the dreariest and most bitter failure but also of life-giving fulfillment: marriage is all these things because it is the place where the greatest thing in heaven and earth breaks through into our lives, the hard baffling outcrop of what we call love. It is all these things at once because it is the point, mysterious and yet always inescapably there, at which flesh and spirit meet, struggle, perceive and recognize each other, so that they merge in a unity without end or stand opposed in a hatred without pity. It is the place where our condition is made clear, is lit up, where we suffer distress and return to peace; the point at which we take, or refuse to take, our place in the procession that never ends; the caravan whose journey has no stopping place, our place which, however humble, can belong to no one else in the simple yet mysterious business which is called life.

— Jean De Fabregues, *Christian Marriage*

Chapter 5.

MESSAGES TO A WIFE

If the man is the head of the family,
    the woman is the heart,
    and as he occupies the chief place in ruling,
    so she may and ought to claim for herself
    the chief place in love.

— Pope Pius XI, *Casti Connubii,*
December 31, 1930

A Wife's Daily Prayer: "As a wife, I beseech Thee, O Triune God, make me cheerful, trustful, unselfish, thrifty, and an affectionate companion. If I am blessed with Motherhood, I ask the additional grace of patience and good example. May our family be modeled upon the Holy Family. Amen."

— William T. Mulloy, Bishop of Covington

Behind every great man there is a woman.

— Unknown

SPECIAL PRAYER FOR BRIDE IN NUPTIAL MASS

O God, who by Thy mighty power didst
make all things out of nothing,
Who having set in order the elements of the
universe and made man to God's image,
didst appoint woman to be his
inseparable helpmeet,
in such wise that the woman's body took its
beginning out of the flesh of man,
thereby teaching that what Thou hadst been
pleased to institute from one principle
might never lawfully be put asunder;
O God who hast hallowed wedlock by a
mystery so excellent
that in the marriage bond
Thou didst foreshadow the union of Christ
with His Church . . .
look in Thy mercy upon this Thy handmaid,
who is to be joined in wedlock
and entreats protection and strength
from Thee.

— Roman Missal (Gregorian, 7th century)

Because of their age-long training in human re-lations — for that is what feminine intuition re-ally is — women have a special contribution to make to any group enterprise, and I feel it is up to them to contribute the kinds of awareness that relatively few men . . . have incorporated through their education.

— Margaret Mead, *Blackberry Winter*

Tell my sisters to love the Lord and be satisfied with their husbands in flesh and spirit. In the same way tell my brothers in the name of Jesus Christ to love their wives as the Lord does the Church.

— St. Ignatius of Antioch,
Letter to Polycarp, 5 (2nd century)

A rebellious son is a calamity to his father, and a nagging wife annoys: like a constant dripping.

— Proverbs 19:13,
The Way, Complete Catholic Edition Bible

The husband is the head of the family, the wife its heart and soul. It is only in the Christian family that the wife enjoys that dignity and respect which God originally intended her to have when He made her the companion and helpmate of her husband, not his slave.

— Father John Laux, M.A., *Catholic Morality*

Wives should regard their husbands as they regard the Lord since as Christ is the head of the Church and saves the whole body, so is a husband the head of his wife; and as the Church submits to Christ, so should wives to their husbands, in everything.

— Ephesians 5:22-24, *The Jerusalem Bible*

If you love, you will suffer,
and if you do not love,
you do not know the meaning
of a Christian life.

— Agatha Christie, *An Autobiography*

There are a number of things that submission does not require of a wife. It does not mean that she is a slave or a nonperson without a thought, wish, or desire of her own. She does not have to put on blinders and ignore the faults or behaviors in her husband which may contradict God's Word. It does not mean denying her giftedness and talents. In fact, there will be many occasions in which a wife has greater wisdom, insight, or ability than her husband. When this is the case, the partner with the most to give should have the opportunity to do so.

. . . Submission simply means arranging oneself under the authority of another. Because of abilities and giftedness, this can shift back and forth between partners. This attitude is vital in the marital relationship. Resistance, resentment, and rebellion allow no place for love and intimacy to grow. Biblical submission calls for the wife to trust, respect, and honor her husband from her heart. Submitting to a husband is also an act of submission to the Lord. This is not man's plan but God's.

— H. Norman Wright,
Quiet Times for Couples

Happy the husband of a really good wife;
    the number of his days will be doubled.
A perfect wife is the joy of her husband,
    he will outlive the years of his life in peace.
A good wife is the best of portions,
    reserved for those who fear the Lord;
rich or poor, they will be glad of heart,
    cheerful of face, whatever the season.
The grace of a wife will charm her husband,
    her accomplishments will make him the
        stronger.
A silent wife is a gift from the Lord,
    no price can be put on a well-trained character.
A modest wife is a boon twice over,
    a chaste character cannot be weighed on
        scales.
Like the sun rising over the mountains of the
        Lord
    is the beauty of a good wife in a well-kept
        house.

              — *The Book of Sirach* (26:1-4, 16-21),
              The Jerusalem Bible

When I was young and free and my imagination had no limits, I dreamed of changing the world. As I grew older and wiser, I discovered the world would not change, so I shortened my sights somewhat and decided to change only my country. But it, too, seemed immovable.

As I grew into my twilight years, in one last desperate attempt, I settled for changing only my family, those closest to me, but alas, they would have none of it.

And now as I lie on my deathbed, I suddenly realize: *If I had only changed myself first,* then by example I would have changed my family. From their inspiration and encouragement, I would then have been able to better my country and, who knows, I may have even changed the world (Anonymous, written on tomb of Anglican Bishop in the crypt of Westminster Abbey).

— Jack Canfield and Mark Hansen,
Chicken Soup for the Soul

Better to live on a corner of the roof than share a house with a quarrelsome wife.

— Proverbs 21:9,
Book of Religious Proverbs

A warm hug, a tender squeeze of the hand, a tear wiped from a cheek — these are acts of intimacy. How can anyone be intimate without touching?

— Edward Crowther, *Intimacy*

Do you release your partner to discover his or her hidden potential which has yet to emerge? Your partner belongs to the Lord, and He wants the best for both of you.

Perhaps your partner needs a little more cheering on from you. Perhaps he or she needs a phone call or a personal note from you which says, "go for it; you can do it. I'm here for you; I believe in you; Give it a try; I'm praying for you." These are the kinds of words that cheer a person on. Make cheerleading a consistent pattern in your marriage relationship.

— H. Norman Wright,
Quiet Times for Couples

A wife of noble character is her husband's crown,
but a disgraceful wife is like decay in his bones.
— Proverbs 12:4,
Book of Religious Proverbs

A virtuous wife is a man's greatest treasure.

— Hadith, 418 (Islam)

You are my true and honorable wife,
 As dear to me as are the ruddy drops
 That visit my sad heart.

— William Shakespeare,
Julius Ceasar, II, i, 288

THE SERENITY PRAYER
God grant me the
Serenity to accept the things I cannot change,
Courage to change the things I can, and
Wisdom to know the difference.

— Reinhold Niebuhr, 1943

Catch him [your husband] in the act of doing
what you want him to do and reward him in
some way. . . . Let him know you appreciate what
he's doing. Compliment him, hug him, write him
a note.

— Michele Weiner-Davis, *Changing Her Man*

Why did the Lord make man first and woman thereafter?

Because after He saw Adam, He realized man needed some help.

— Anecdote

Marrying a man is like buying something you've been admiring for a long time in a shop window. You may love it when you get it home, but it doesn't always go with everything else in the house.

— Jean Kerr, American Playwright,
The Snake Has All the Lines
"The Ten Worst Things About a Man" (1959)

To be deeply in love, of course, is a great liberating force and the most common experience that frees. . . . Ideally, both members of a couple in love free each other to new and different worlds. I was no exception to the general rule. The sheer fact of finding myself loved was unbelievable and changed my world, my feelings about life and myself. I was given confidence, strength, and almost a new character.

— Anne Morrow Lindbergh,
quoted in *Quiet Time for Couples*

Chapter 6.

MESSAGES TO A HUSBAND

A BRIDEGROOM'S PRAYER

O heavenly Father, on this, my Wedding Day, I sense as never before Thy sacred Presence. It seems like the first glorious Sabbath in Paradise, when all was good and beautiful, when the universe lay at Thy feet in reverent awe, when the first man and the first woman listened to Thy voice in their pristine joy and innocence.

Behold, the woman Thou gavest me as my companion for this life's journey kneels trustfully at my side. I thank Thee for joining our paths and for granting us the privilege of sharing Thy power in perpetuating the work of Thy Hands. I know that she is Thy gift to me, and I vow in my deepest soul to love her, treasure her, and keep her with unswerving fidelity until my dying breath. May the love which knits our souls together today never lose its ardor, its charm, its sweetness, and may spiritual wisdom and maturer understanding ever strengthen our holy bond as the days roll by, and as the bloom and vigor of youth give way to the infirmities of advancing years.

In joy and sorrow, in triumph and failure, I will stand by her side not as her lord and master, but as a devoted friend and protector, sharing with her lovingly all I have and hold. I will build her a home, enduring beautiful, peaceful: she shall be my queen. My comfort, the pride of my life. Over this home we will write the Holy name of Jesus. Grant, O Heavenly Father, that the charm of this beautiful Cana Day may abide in it forever, and that pure love which He bore to His Bride, our Holy Church; and as he presented "to Himself the church in all her glory, not having spot or wrinkle or any such thing," so may I be permitted someday to present to Thee this bride of mine to whom I have pledged constant fidelity before Thy altar.

O Father, this the prayer of my heart. Bless us and keep us in Thy holy grace. Amen.

— Father John O'Brien, *Happy Marriage*

There as my heart is set, there will I wive.
— William Chaucer, *The Clerk's Tale*
(14th century)

And you husbands, show the same kind of love to your wives as Christ showed to the Church when He died for her, to make her holy and clean, washed by baptism and God's Word; so that he could give her to himself as a glorious church without a single spot or wrinkle or blemish, being holy and without a single fault. That is how husbands should treat their wives, loving them as parts of themselves.

— Ephesians 5:25-29,
The Way, Complete Catholic Edition Bible

I would give up all my genius and all my books if there were only some woman, somewhere, who cared whether or not I came home late for dinner.

— Ivan Turgenev, Russian Novelist

Every day I re-choose my wife by my actions, through my words and thoughts. It isn't dramatic but it is a conscious reaffirmation of my love for her, a conscious appreciation of her love for me, and a fresh determination to deepen that commitment that gives our partnership its fire and its staying power.

— Alanson B. Houghton, *Partners in Love*

The Christian way to exercise authority is to serve. Christ-like authority is not absolute control over another human being; it is not making unilateral decisions and transmitting them to another to carry out; it is not reducing another to the status of a slave. To be head as Christ is head is to serve. The Christian husband, as Markus Barth puts it so beautifully, is called to be "the first servant of his wife," and she is equally called to be his first servant.

— Michael G. Lawler, *Marriage and Sacrament*

A man should never forget that one of the greatest needs of a woman is her need for affection. Women tend to be lonely more than men do. Therefore, the wise husband, who is aware of this, will offset that loneliness with frequent acts of affection, small ones, but creative ones.

— Martin G. Olsen, Ed.D. and
George E. Von Kaenel, S.J., *Two as One*

Honor your wife and your life will be enriched.
—Talmud (Judaism)

Let me not to the marriage of true minds
Admit impediments: love is not love
Which alters when it alteration finds,
Or bends with the remover to remove.
Oh no! It is an ever-fixed mark
That looks on tempests and is never shaken;
It is the star to every wandering bark,
Whose worth's unknown although his height
be taken.
Love's not Time's fool, though rosy
lips and cheeks
Within his bending sickle's compass come;
Love alters not with his brief hours and weeks,
But bears it out even to the edge of doom.
If this be error and upon me proved,
I never writ, nor man ever loved.
— William Shakespeare, *Sonnet* CXVI

A father can give his sons homes and riches, but
only the Lord can give them understanding wives.
— Proverbs 19:14,
The Way, Complete Catholic Edition Bible

Joseph became the husband of Mary only after he had given up his plan to marry her. This is all about loss and finding of Mary. It parallels the loss and finding of Jesus in the Temple. Joseph had his heart set on living with Mary as his wife. When her mysterious pregnancy broke up his plan, he decided that he had to give up the vision he had formed for his life — his plan of serving God with Mary as his wife. . . . Every true seeker of God, from the beginning of time to the end of the world, has to pass through this mysterious death and rebirth, perhaps many times over. Joseph's love of Mary and his vision of life with her — and later his love of Jesus and his vision of life with him — were his two great visions, both given to him by God and both seemingly taken away from him by circumstances God had arranged. These were the two eyes that he had to give up in order to see with God's eyes. He had to surrender his personal vision in order to become *Vision itself*. That, after all, is the goal and term of Christian life.

— Father Thomas Keating, O.C.S.O., *Awakenings*

St. Joseph truly is the silent figure of the New Testament. For instance, the Gospel does not record one spoken verse for St. Joseph. Nevertheless, what this great saint did in his life for God speaks volumes. . . . St. Matthew identifies Joseph as an "upright man." The original text uses the word *just* or *righteous,* which better reflects that he lived by God's standard, keeping the commandment and emulating God's love. . . . St. Joseph fulfilled his obligations courageously. . . . Throughout the Gospel he faithfully and unquestioningly obeyed the commands of God; taking his family to the safety of Egypt to flee the wrath of King Herod; returning to Nazareth; presenting his child in the Temple for circumcision and formal presentation; and traveling to Jerusalem to celebrate Passover. . . . He accepted the responsibility of his vocation — being faithful spouse and father. He provided the best he could for his family, whether that meant the stable in Bethlehem or the home in Nazareth.

 . . . Pope Pius IX declared him [Joseph] the patron of the Catholic Church in 1870.

— Father William Saunders,
"Straight Answers: St. Joseph,"
Arlington Catholic Herald, March 19, 1998

Husbands, love your wives,
   and avoid any bitterness toward them.
                              — Colossians 3:19,
                              The New American Bible

   Blessed are you, O God of our fathers;
      praised be your name forever and ever.
Let the heavens and all your creation
   praise you forever.
You made Adam and you gave him his wife Eve
   to be his help and support;
   and from these two the human race descended.
You said, "It is not good for the man to be alone;
   let us make him a partner like himself."
Now, LORD, you know that I take this wife of
      mine
   not because of lust,
   but for a noble purpose.
Call down your mercy on me and on her,
   and allow us to live together
      to a happy old age.
                              — Tobit 8:5-7,
                              The New American Bible

St. Joseph is the perfect role model for both spouse and father, and we should honor and emulate him.

— Unknown, *Sermon,* March 19,
Feast of St. Joseph

Woman is not independent of man or man of woman in the Lord. For just as woman came from man, so man is born of woman; but all things are from God.

— 1 Corinthians 11:11-12,
The New American Bible

He who finds a wife finds what is good and receives favor from the Lord.

— Proverbs 18:22,
Book of Religious Proverbs

He who loves his wife as himself, honors her more than himself.

— Talmud

Between a man and his wife, nothing ought to rule but love.

> — William Penn,
> *Some Fruits of Solitude*, 1693

Before marriage man hovers above life, observes it from without; only in marriage does he plunge into it, entering it through the personality of another.

> — Alexander Yelchaninov,
> *Fragments of a Diary*, 1881-1934

. . . She is mine own,
And I as rich in having such a jewel
As twenty seas, if all their sand were pearl,
The water nectar, and the rocks pure gold.

> — William Shakespeare,
> *Two Gentlemen of Verona*

Of the influences which shape one's life,
nothing comes into the same category with
the great crowning influence
which man possesses in that perfect partner —
a well-mated wife.
To have one by you
who shares with head and heart
successes and failures;
who gives due encouragement,
but has the courage to drive home truth,
unpalatable but necessary sometimes,
such a partner is beyond praise or price.
She is simply one's needed lifeblood
and I make no apology
for this due tribute to mine.
— Viscount Cowdray, *Happy Marriage*

Chapter 7.

ENCOUNTERING LIFE'S DIFFICULTIES

No problem which any married couple can have is beyond solution if they are willing to get down on their knees together and ask God what to do about it. It is not a question of what the husband wants — or what the wife wants — but always, what does God want?

> — Peter Marshall, *The Best of Peter Marshall*

Wisdom is learning what to overlook.

> — William James

And I will give you a new heart — I will give you new and right desires — and put a new spirit within you. I will take out your stony hearts of sin and give you new hearts of love.

> — Ezekiel 36:26,
> *The Way, Complete Catholic Edition Bible*

People ask me what advice I have
for a married couple struggling in their
relationship.
I always answer
"Pray and forgive";
and to young people who come from
violent homes,
"Pray and forgive";
and to the single mother with no
family support,
"Pray and forgive."
You can say,
"My Lord, I love You.
My God, I am sorry.
My God, I believe in You.
My God, I trust You.
Help us to love one another
as You love us."

— Mother Teresa,
Meditations From A Simple Path

In the end we are always left with the same painful emptiness which we were led to believe we
could fill.

— John Powell, S.J. , *Unconditional Love*

For no love is free from periods of difficulties. But (as Kierkegaard aptly remarks), because it implies will, commitment, duty, and responsibility, marriage braces spouses to *fight* to save the precious gift of their love. It gives them the glorious confidence that with God's help, they will overcome the difficulties and emerge victorious. Thus, by adding a formal element to the material element of love, marriage guarantees the future of love and protects it against the temptations which are bound to arise in human existence.

— Dietrich Von Hildebrand,
Marriage: The Mystery of Faithful Love

The plain fact is that
most of us do not take marriage seriously.
We get so caught up in all the other demands
that our marriage
and the quality of our togetherness
fall to the bottom of our
"to do" list.

— Drs. Evelyn and Paul Moschetta,
The Marriage Spirit

The ideas of "me" and "mine" are at the root of all conflict.

— Nisargadatta

Among the difficulties, the shocks, the lusts that may lie along the path of life, your two souls, inseparably joined, will be neither alone nor defenseless; the all-powerful grace of God, which is the proper fruit of the sacrament, will always be with you, to uphold your weakness at each step, to sweeten all sacrifices, to comfort and console throughout all trials, even the hardest. If in order to obey the divine law you must reject the earthly joys of which you catch a glimpse in times of temptation, if you must renounce the attempt to make a new life, grace will be there to bring back to you in all their force the promises of our faith, the knowledge that the only true life, the life we must never endanger, is the life of heaven. . . .

— Pope Pius XII, *The Laws of Christian Married Life, Address to Young Couples*, April 22, 1942

Much marriage difficulty and unhappiness are due to the failure of partners to accept the fact of their finiteness and its meaning.

Instead, they hold themselves up to ideals of performance possible only to God.

— Reul Howe, *Sex and Religion Today*

For all my good intentions, there are days when things go wrong or I fall into old habits. When things are not going well, when I'm grumpy or mad, I'll realize that I've not been paying attention to my soul and I've not been following my best routine.

— Robert Fulghum, *Handbook for the Soul*

Seldom or never does a marriage develop into
an individual relationship
smoothly and without crises.
There is no birth of consciousness
without pain.

— C.G. Jung,
Marriage as a Psychological Relationship

The motto of the follower of Christ must be, "Keep going ahead. Don't look back." If our Lord Jesus Christ had been someone preoccupied with his own hurt feelings, none of us would have been saved. Mercifully, God does not nurse hurt feelings. For our own spiritual, as well as psychological good, we must forgive those who trespass against us.

— Father Benedict J. Groeschel, C.F.R.,
Arise from Darkness

If your marriage is not daily being born
it is dying . . .
Love is an activity, not a passion.
Its essence is to "labor" for someone
To make someone grow.
To love a person productively implies
To care and feel responsible
For the development of all his human powers.
— John L. Thomas, S.J.,
Beginning Your Marriage

These books [paperback romance novels] sell because at some level we all long for this [the ideal romance]. We want to be discovered under our façade; to be understood, cherished, and delighted in; to be known in our most hidden places, and to have everything that is known loved. We want someone who is "all there is to me;" someone who, like Kenny Rogers' song, *Lady*, "will come into my life and make me whole."

We cannot do this for each other.

As Sebastian Moore says, "we are limited by our own boundaries, our awarenesses. We cannot get inside, interior, to another. We cannot meet totally." We try sometimes, we try hard, but even in the best of these attempts we cannot sustain it completely. . . . The best of our moments of union are followed by the awareness of the other as separate. And if we expect the other to complete us forever, we can only be frustrated. Expecting that of the other dooms the relationship. There is one who can complete us, one who can be experienced as totally inward, knowing us from within as no one else can. There is one who has no limits, no boundaries, who is all there is to me. One whom I am made for. And this, Thomas Aquinas would say, is the one we call God.

— Patricia Livingston, *Lessons of the Heart*

The Desire for Happiness

The Beatitudes respond to the natural desire for happiness. This desire is of divine origin: God has placed it in the human heart in order to draw man to the One who alone can fulfill it:

> We all want to live happily; in the whole human race there is no one who does not assent to this proposition, even before it is fully articulated (St. Augustine, *De moribus eccl.* 1,3,4, PL 32, 1312).

> How is it, then, that I seek you, Lord? Since in seeking you, my God, I seek a happy life, let me seek you so that my soul may live, for my body draws life from my soul and my soul draws life from you (St. Augustine, *Conf.* 10, 20: PL 32, 791).

> God alone satisfies (St. Thomas Aquinas, *Expos. in symb. apost.* 1).

— *Catechism of the Catholic Church*, 1718

Marriage is the most inviolable and irrevocable of all contracts that were ever formed. Every human compact may be lawfully dissolved but this.

— James Cardinal Gibbons,
The Faith of our Fathers, 31 (19th century)

Marriage as a Psychological Relationship

Where did this superstition begin that married persons are going to find happiness ready made? Happiness is a result of struggle. Happiness is something you work out for yourself and work out chiefly by forgetting self and serving others. Who in this world has a right to it without the slow, painful struggle toward God?

Marriage is a job.

No marriage is a successful marriage which could not have ended in failure.

But make it a success and you will become a ripened soul who knows where to find happiness and what it is. Marriage is not a shallow human joy but a great means of grace, a way to heaven.

— Kathleen Norris,
After the Honeymoon — What?

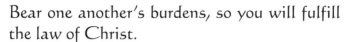

Bear one another's burdens, so you will fulfill the law of Christ.

— Galatians 6:2,
The New American Bible

Love has a hem to her garment that reaches to the very dust. It sweeps the stains from the streets and lanes, and because it can, it must.

— Mother Teresa,
Contemplative in the Heart of the World, 1985

In a nutshell, the fact that marriage is a Sacrament means it is indissoluble. You just don't get divorced. That provides a very, very solid backbone for a Catholic marriage.

There will, of course, be tough times to get through — *everyone* goes through that. But because of the indissolubility, we stick it out, we make it work — easy or not. That gives us an *enormous* edge. It is both an asset to the man and to the woman in a Catholic marriage.

— Anonymous (Married forty-six years;
four children; two grandchildren.)

The most exhausting thing in life is being in-sincere.

— Anne Morrow Lindberg,
A Gift from the Sea, chapter 2, 1955

It is easier to seek a little pleasure here, a little love there, than to resist the first demand of the senses which say: change! But it is through victory over these first troubles and traps that love grows deeper. A man who stops digging at the first stone in his way has not cultivated his soil enough for it to bring him a harvest. Like all human work, love does not bear fruit without long labour. He who refuses to labour long will never know the true fruit of love which transforms his very soul.

But he who sets himself to the slow business of building up love will see its grandeur rise above obstacles and sufferings, just as the traveller on a mountain road sees new horizons unfold as each crest is reached, at each turn of the road. But unless he is willing to accept the long, upward struggle, the horizon will be hidden from view.

— Jean De Fabregues, *Christian Marriage*

. . . There is another kind of suffering few of us can flee. And that we cannot stop by a mere act of will: not by averting our eyes, running away, slamming the door.

The agony of love in all its variations.

Man and woman love. The many aspects of love between male and female . . . Anxiety about the one so close to us . . . Long separations . . . Conflicts, quarrels, doubts . . . other . . . Indifference . . . The bitter wounds of unfaithfulness . . . To be denied the person most deeply loved . . . The awful unfilled hungers of body and soul . . .

These our private crucifixions.

. . . You [God] make me realize that anyone who drinks from the sweet cup of love must also swallow the gall. But love is worth it . . . ah, but it's worth it! And if you are truly love, as Jesus taught, then the price we pay for love has even more value.

In suffering for love of others we are also suffering for love of you. This suffering I welcome, Lord.

— Marjorie Holmes,
To Help You Through the Hurting

A lot of people today are signing contracts —
you know, pre-nuptial contracts — already de-
ciding before they get married that it might not
work. But when we got married, we realized we
were in it for the long haul, and I do think that
we realized that it's a Sacrament . . . and that's
a very unique thought.

> — Anonymous (Married thirty-six years;
> four children; six grandchildren)

Working through difficult times can lead to a
stronger and more meaningful relationship.

> — Jeanette and Robert Lauer,
> *Till Death Do Us Part*

Life is too short to waste
In critic peep or cynic bark,
Quarrel or reprimand;
'Twill soon be dark;
Up! mind thine own aim, and
God save the mark!

— Ralph Waldo Emerson, *Poems, To J.W.,* 1847

In my work at the Roma Rota [the highest court in the Catholic Church], I not infrequently come across petitions of annulment of what clearly are perfectly genuine marriages of couples who married out of love, but whose marriages collapsed fundamentally because they deliberately delayed having children and thus deprived their married love of its natural support.

If two people remain just looking ecstatically into each other's eyes, the defects that little by little they are going to discover there can eventually begin to appear intolerable. If they gradually learn to look *out* together at their children, they will still discover each other's defects, but they will have less time or reason to think them intolerable. They cannot, however, look out together at what is not there.

Conjugal love, then, needs the support represented by children.

> — Cormac Burke, *Covenanted Happiness:*
> *Love and Commitment in Marriage*

Oh love, as long as you can love.
> — Ferdinand Freiligrath, *Der Liebe Dauer,* 1830

Love conquers all things; let us too surrender to Love.

— Virgil, *Ecologues*, X, l.69

The way I see it,
if you want the rainbow,
You gotta put up with the rain.

— Dolly Parton

Chapter 8.

SHARING IN LIFE'S JOYS

Be happy in the moment, that's enough.
Each moment is all we need, not more.
Be happy now and if you show through your
actions
that you love others,
including those who are poorer than you,
you'll give them happiness, too.
It doesn't take much —
it can be just giving a smile.
The world would be a much better place
if everyone smiled more.
So smile,
be cheerful,
be joyous that God loves you.

— Mother Teresa,
Meditations From A Simple Path

Love to faults is always blind,
Always is to joy inclined,
Lawless, winged, and unconfined,
And breaks all chains from every mind.

— William Blake, *Love to Faults*

To make marriage a go, love must touch the qualities of each mate and integrate them into the richer and fuller personalities born in the womb of matrimony. "God," says an old Portuguese proverb, "writes straight with crooked lines." Love is the essence of God and thus partakes of His mysterious power. It is the miracle and the mystery of love that blends the separate notes of each partner, which alone sound off-key, into the glorious symphony of life in whose overtones and undertones one catches ever and anon the lilting melody of love's mystic song.

— Father John A. O'Brien, *Happy Marriage*

O, my Luve is like a red, red rose,
That's newly sprung in June.
O, my Luve is like the melodie,
That's sweetly played in tune.

— Robert Burns,
A Red, Red Rose

There's no place like home.

— Dorothy, *The Wizard of Oz*

If the only prayer you say in your whole life is "thank you," that would suffice.

> — Meister Eckhart,
> quoted in *Running on Empty*

The efficient cause of matrimony is the mutual consent of the partners expressed in words about their undertaking here and now. Marriage has three blessings. The first is children, to be received and raised for God's service. The second is the loyal faith whereby each serves the other. The third is the sacrament, which signifies the inseparable union of Christ with His Church.

> — St. Thomas Aquinas: *Concerning the Articles of Faith and Sacraments of the Church*, 2.

If solid happiness we prize,
within our breast this jewel lies,
And they are fools who roam; the world has
Nothing to bestow,
From our own selves our bliss must flow,
And that dear hut — our home.

> — Nathaniel Cotton

There is only one happiness in life, to love and be loved.

— George Sand, *Letter to Lina Calamatta,*
March 31, 1862

Love consists in this, that two solitudes protect and touch and greet each other.

— Rainer Maria Rilke, *Letters to a Young Poet*

At the beautiful Nuptial Mass the couple receives not only the special blessing of God on their marriage but also the greatest gift within His power to bestow — our Blessed Lord and Savior, Jesus Christ, in Holy Communion. His strong arms will hold the couple together for life in a holy union of love and happiness. To that home we can apply the words of Christ: "And the rain fell, and the floods came, and the winds blew; and they beat upon that house, and it fell not; for it was founded on a rock."

And the rock is Christ.

— Father John A. O'Brien, *Happy Marriage*

A marriage based on full confidence, based on complete and unqualified frankness on both sides; they are not keeping anything back; there's no deception underneath it all. If I might so put it, it's an agreement for the mutual forgiveness of sin.

— Henrik Ibsen, *The Wild Duck*

No one who lights a lamp hides it away or places it [under a bushel basket], but on a lampstand so that those who enter might see the light.

— Luke 11:33,
The New American Bible

Joys shared are doubled;
    Sorrows shared are halved.

— Old Proverb (Unknown origin)

Life's greatest happiness is to be convinced we are loved.

— Victor Hugo, *Les Miserables*

. . . Joy is not just a quality radiating from individual persons. It is as much, if not more so, a gift to the community of believers. "Where two or three meet in my name, I shall be there with them" (Mt 18:20). These words reveal that the ecstatic joy of the house of love is Christ's own joy-filled presence, made manifest each time we enter into communion with each other in and through Christ.

— Henri J.M. Nouwen, *Lifesigns*

The best gift one friend can give to another is prayer.

— Cardinal Terence Cooke (familiar saying of)

It is a lovely thing to have a husband and wife developing together and having the feeling of falling in love again. That is what marriage really means: helping one another to reach the full status of being persons, responsible and autonomous beings who do not run away from life.

— Paul Tournier

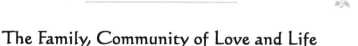

The Family, Community of Love and Life

Jesus was invited to Cana of Galilee to take part in a wedding and marriage feast. We may rightly deduce from the evangelist's text that this episode in particular determined the beginning of his apostolic life, even though various other events are linked with the commencement of Jesus of Nazareth's public activity. It is important to note that Jesus began His work in the circumstances of a wedding.

At the very beginning of His *messianic mission,* Jesus Christ in a certain sense touches *human life at its fundamental point.* The starting point. Matrimony marks a new beginning every time, even though it is as ancient as humanity. This is above all, the beginning of a new community bearing the name "family." The family is the community of love and life. So the mystery of human life was entrusted to it by the Creator. Matrimony is the beginning of the new community of love and life upon which man's future on earth depends.

— Pope John Paul,
from *Prayers and Devotions From John Paul II*

Someone asked me to name the time
Our friendship stopped and love began.
Oh, my darling, that's the secret.
Our friendship never stopped.
— Lois Wyse, *Love Poems for the Very Married*

There's no surprise more magical than the surprise of being loved: it is God's finger on man's shoulder.
— Charles Morgan,
American Heritage Dictionary of American Quotes

There is a comfort in the strength of love;
'Twill make a thing endurable, which else
would overset the brain, or break the heart.
— William Wordsworth, *Michael, I.,* 448

Two souls with but a single thought,
Two hearts that beat as one.
— Maria Lovell, *Ingomar the Barbarian*

The human condition has been compared to a person trapped at the bottom of a deep dry well. All calls for help go unanswered.

They seem to be blown away by the winds that howl at the top of the well.

Hope begins to wear thin. Then, when hope seems certainly to be on its deathbed, an answering call comes from the top of the well:

"We know that you are down there. We are coming with help. We will rescue you." There is an explosion of joy in the heart of the trapped person.

"Thank God, someone finally knows that I am here!"

— John Powell, S.J., *Happiness Is an Inside Job*

This is one of the miracles of love: it gives . . . a power of seeing through its own enchantments and yet not being disenchanted.

— C.S. Lewis,
American Heritage Dictionary of American Quotes

Same old slippers,
Same old rice,
Same old glimpse of
Paradise.
— Philip Larkin, *Self's the Man*

It is in the shelter of each other
that the people live.

— Irish Proverb

Time was away and somewhere else,
There were two glasses and two chairs
And two people with one pulse.
— Louis MacNeice, *Meeting Point*

Unshared joy is an unlighted candle.

— Spanish Proverb

There is no more lovely, friendly, and charming relationship, communion, or company than a good marriage.

— Martin Luther

There is no remedy for love,
    but more love.

— Henry D. Thoreau, *Journal,* July 25, 1839

He who leaves his house in search of happiness pursues a shadow.

— Unknown

A husband, a good marriage, is earth.

— Anne Morrow Lindbergh,
Diaries and Letters, 1944

How do I love thee? Let me count the ways.
I love thee to the depth and breadth
and height
My soul can reach, when feeling out of sight
For the ends of Being and ideal Grace.
I love thee to the level of every day's
Most quiet need, by sun and candle-light.
I love thee freely, as men strive for Right;
I love thee purely, as they turn from Praise.
I love thee with the passion put to use
In my old griefs,
and with my childhood's faith.
I love thee with a love I seemed to lose
With my lost saints — I love thee
with the breath,
Smiles, tears, of all my life! — and,
if God choose,
I shall but love thee better after death.

— Elizabeth Barrett Browning,
Sonnets from the Portuguese, 43

Family life is the source of the greatest human
happiness.

— Robert J. Gavigurst

Laughter in the Walls

I pass a lot of houses on my way home —
    some pretty,
        some expensive,
            some inviting —
but my heart always skips a beat
        When I turn down the road
and see my house nestled against the hill.
    I guess I'm especially proud
of the house and the way it looks because
    I drew the plans myself.
It started out large enough for us —
    I even had a study —
two teenaged boys now reside in there.
    And it had a guest room —
my girl and nine dolls are permanent guests.
    It had a small room Peg
had hoped would be her sewing room —
    the two boys swinging on the dutch door
have claimed this room as their own.
    So it really doesn't look right now
as if I'm much of an architect.
    But it will get larger again —
one by one they will go away
    to work,
        to college,
            To their own houses,

and then there will be room —
     a guest room,
          a study,
     and a sewing room
     for just the two of us.
But it won't be empty —
     every corner
          every room
               every nick
                    in the coffee table
will be crowded with memories.
Memories of picnics,
     parties, Christmases,
          bedside vigils, summers,
               fires, winters, going barefoot,
     leaving for vacation, cats,
          conversations, black eyes,
     graduations, first dates,
          ball games, arguments,
     washing dishes, bicycles,
          dogs, boat rides,
     getting home from vacation,
          meals, rabbits and
     a thousand other things
          that fill the lives
     of those who would raise five.
And Peg and I will sit
     quietly by the fire
     and listen to the
     laughter in the walls.
                    — Bob Benson, *Laughter in the Walls*

Chapter 9.

FAMILY ISSUES

Children, obey your parents; this is the right thing to do because God has placed them in authority over you. . . . And now a word to you parents. Don't keep on scolding and nagging your children, making them angry and resentful. Rather, bring them up with the loving discipline the Lord himself approves, with suggestions and godly advice.

> — Ephesians 6:1-4,
> *The Way, Complete Catholic Edition Bible*

Whosoever being rich does not support mother and father when old and past their youth, let one know him as an outcast.

> — *Sutta Nipata*, 123 (Buddhism)

Christ is the Head of this Household,
The Unseen Guest at Every Meal,
The Silent Auditor of Every Spoken Word.

> — Motto

You want your child to feel safe at home. [But] You also want to prepare him for the world, which does not love unquestioningly.

— Peggy Noonan, *How Much Should a Parent Push?*

The family is one of nature's masterpieces.

— George Santayana, *The Life of Reason*, vol. 2, "Reason in Society," 1905

When we cannot see our way,
Let us trust and still obey.

— J.C. MaCaulay

A Song for Hearth and Home

Dark is the night, and fitful and drearily
     Rushes the wind, the waves of the sea!
Little care I, as here I sit cheerily,
     Wife at my side and baby on knee:
King, king, crown me the king:
     home is the kingdom and love is the king!

— William Rankin Duryear,
in *Happy Marriage*

As the family goes, so goes the nation!
> —Pope John Paul II, *Family:*
> *The Most Vital Foundation of Society;*
> Delivered at Trans World Dome,
> January 27, 1999

When you take your rightful place in the family — if you are married, then you create a relationship with your wife that is not based on subservience but rather on mutual respect and mutual submission to each other and to the Lord. It means that you make your marriage the sacrament that it is supposed to be and tell you children: "As for me and my house, we are going to serve the Lord" (Joshua 24:15).
> — Raymond Lee Harris, Jr.

Discipline your son in his early years while there is hope. If you don't you will ruin his life.
> — Proverbs 19:18,
> *The Way, Complete Catholic Edition Bible*

Children Learn What They Live

If a child lives with criticism,
He learns to condemn.
If a child lives with hostility,
he learns to fight.
If a child lives with ridicule,
He learns to be shy.
If a child lives with shame,
He learns to feel guilty.
If a child lives with tolerance,
He learns to be patient.
If a child lives with encouragement,
He learns confidence.
If a child lives with praise,
he learns to appreciate.
If a child lives with fairness,
he learns justice.
If a child lives with security,
He learns to have faith.
If a child lives with approval,
He learns to like himself.
If a child lives with acceptance, and friendship,
He learns to find love in the world.

— Dorothy Law Nolte

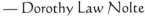

TenCommandments
for a Happy Marriage (Family)

1. Thou shalt make thy promise of mutual love and loyalty a vow to God, binding until death.
2. Thou shalt abstain from the angry word which wounds more deeply than a sword.
3. Thou shalt respect the personality of they mate and not seek to dominate or tyrannize.
4. Thou shalt allow no in-laws to interfere with the running of the home.
5. Thou shalt abstain from drink where alcohol is a danger to either party.
6. Thou shalt make a family budget and observe it.
7. Thou shalt eschew pettiness, nagging, selfishness, jealousy, and false pride.
8. Thou shalt grow in consideration and love each day and share thy interests and pleasures to a maximum.
9. Thou shalt love thy children as God's supreme gift and rear them to be good citizens with a sense of humor, tolerance, and fair play.
10. Thou shalt kneel together in prayer each night, knowing that the family that prays together stays together.

— Father John A. O'Brien, *Happy Marriage*

The good of a stable home or haven: of knowing that this "belongingness" — shared with others — is for keeps. People want that, are made for that, expect that it will require sacrifices and sense that the sacrifices are worth it. . . . It is a strange head and heart that rejects the permanence of the marriage relationship.

— John F. Kippley, *Marriage Is for Keeps*

Children constitute the heart of the home.

— Father John A. O'Brien, *Happy Marriage*

Unconditional love corresponds to one of the deepest longings, not only of the child, but of every human being; on the other hand, to be loved because of one's merit, because one deserves it, always leaves doubt; maybe I did not please the person whom I want to love me, maybe this, or that — there is always a fear that love could disappear. Furthermore, "deserved" love easily leaves a bitter feeling that one is not loved for oneself, that one is loved *only* because one pleases, that one is, in the last analysis, not loved at all but used.

— Erich Fromm, *The Art of Loving*

. . . Being married and having children has impressed on my mind certain lessons, and most of what I am forced to learn about myself is not pleasant. The quantity of sheer impenetrable selfishness in the human breast (in my breast) is a never-failing source of wonderment. I do not want to be disturbed, challenged, troubled. Huge regions of myself belong only to me. Seeing myself through the unblinking eyes of an intelligent, honest spouse is humiliating. Trying to act fairly to children, each of whom is temperamentally different from myself and from each other, is baffling. My family bonds hold me back from many opportunities. And yet these bonds are, I know, my liberation. They force me to be a different sort of human being in a way I want and need.

— Michael Novak, *The Family Out of Favor*

If you bungle raising your children,
I don't think whatever else you do
well matters very much.
— Jacqueline Kennedy Onassis,
A Mother's Thoughts

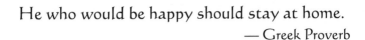

He who would be happy should stay at home.
                            — Greek Proverb

I took on child-rearing not only as a work of love and duty but as a profession that was fully as interesting and challenging as any honorable profession in the world and one that demanded the best that I could bring.
                            — Rose Kennedy,
                            A Mother's Thoughts

. . . "Like mother, like daughter."
                            — Ezekiel 16:44,
                            The New American Bible

It goes without saying that you should never have more children than you have car windows.
                            — Erma Bombeck,
                            A Mother's Thoughts

A Prayer for Every Family

God, from whom all fatherhood in heaven and earth descends, Father, who are Love and Life, ensure that every human family on earth shall become, through Your son, Jesus Christ, "born of woman," and through the Holy Spirit, the source of divine charity, a true shrine of life and love for the generations which are always renewing themselves.

Ensure that Your grace shall guide the thoughts and the words of spouses toward the good of their families and of all families in the world. Ensure that the young generations shall find firm support in the family for their humanity and their growth in truth and love. Ensure that love, reinforced by the grace of the Sacrament of Matrimony shall show itself to be stronger than any weakness and every crisis through which our families pass at times.

Ensure, finally, we ask You, through intercession of the Holy Family of Nazareth, that the Church, in the midst of all the nations of the earth, may fruitfully accomplish her mission in the family and through the family, through Christ Our Lord, who is the way, the truth and the life, for ever and ever. Amen.

— Pope John Paul II,
from *Prayers and Devotions From John Paul II*

Chapter 10.

HAPPY ANNIVERSARY

To wake at dawn with a winged heart and give thanks for another day of loving.

— Kahlil Gibran,
quoted in *Running on Empty*

Arnold Bennett says that the horror of marriage lies in its "dailiness." All acuteness of relationship is rubbed away by this. The truth is more like this: life — say four days out of seven — becomes automatic; but on the fifth day a bead of sensation (between husband and wife) forms which is all the fuller and more sensitive because of the automatic customary unconscious days on either side. That is to say the year is marked by moments of great intensity. Hardy's "moments of vision." How can a relationship endure for any length of time except under these conditions?

— Virginia Woolf, *The Diary of Virginia Woolf*, vol. 3, entry for August 2, 1926

Now is the high-tide of the year,
And whatever of life hath ebbed away
Comes flooding back with ripply cheer
Now the heart is so full that a drop overfills it,
We are happy now, because God wills it.

— James Russell Lowell

Face forward. Rather than look back at losses
you suffered last year, look ahead to plans and
hopes for the year ahead.

— Unknown

Life is like a river. It begins and then pushes on
relentlessly through time until it ends in death
and the new life beyond. As birthdays pass, persons change. Each of us is somewhat different
today from yesterday, this year from last, this
decade from ten years ago.

— Jan and Myron Chartier,
Trusting Together in God

The journey of married people, like that of all human lives, has its stages; difficult and sorrowful moments have their place in it, as you know from your experience through the years.

— Pope Paul VI, *Address*, 1970

Prayer of Spouses for Each Other

Lord Jesus, grant that I and my spouse may have a true and understanding love for each other. Grant that we may both be filled with faith and trust. Give us the grace to live with each other in peace and harmony. May we always bear with one another's weaknesses and grow from each other's strengths. Help us to forgive one another's failings and grant us patience, kindness, cheerfulness and the spirit of placing the well-being of one another ahead of self.

May the love that brought us together grow and mature with each passing year. Bring us both ever closer to You through our love for each other. Let our love grow to perfection. Amen.

— *Prayers for All Occasions* from The Basilica of the National Shrine of the Immaculate Conception, Washington, D.C.

The continuing shifts and challenges of a maturing marriage give it the appearance of a journey. Marriage as a journey suggests that this relationship is not a location in life but a pattern of movement. Marriage is not a place where we live but a way that we travel through life. The image of the journey responds to the sense of the precariousness of marriage. Even after this trek is well begun, we continue to learn new things about our self and our partner. These are often subtle and confusing things, not covered under the contract or the institutional warranty. . . . God is a presence sensed on the trip. God is a presence that visits our life in strange and unpredictable ways to give it meaning and direction. Religious faith and a Christian marriage require our attentiveness to this subtle and graceful presence.

— Evelyn Whitehead and James Whitehead,
Marrying Well

The holiest of all holidays are those
Kept by ourselves in silence and apart,
The secret anniversaries of the heart . . .
— Henry Wadsworth Longfellow, *Holidays*

"Married," from *Living Out Loud*

It's getting on ten years that I've been married. I'm not sure when I realized that reality was going to be both something less and something more.

. . . When I was younger, I tended to fall in love with just one thing: a kind of bravado, a certain smile. (The girl in the doorway, I am convinced, has fallen for blond hair and a crooked grin.) I even fell in love with a certain set of bony shoulders in a sport jacket years ago. But unlike a lot of my friends, who went through more than a few Mr. Wrongs and have now settled down with Mr. Maybe, I married the person inside the sport jacket. And I held on like a dog with a bone to a love affair between a girl whose idea of awesome responsibility was a psych[ology] midterm and a boy who painted his dorm room black, long after that boy and girl were gone. I held onto what was going on in that doorway long past the time when I was really too old to believe in magic.

Truth is, I still believe in magic, and it's still there, although there's no point denying that it is occasionally submerged beneath a welter of cereal bowls, dirty shirts, late nights, early mornings, and all the other everyday things that bubble-gum music never reflects. But what I didn't know about marriage, the less magical parts of it, has become perhaps more important to me. Now we have history as well as chemistry. An enormous part of my past does not exist without my husband. An enormous part of my present, too. I still feel somehow that things do not really happen to me unless I have told them to him. I don't mean this nonsense about being best friends, which I have never been able to cotton to; our relationship is too judgmental, too demanding, too prickly to have much in common with the quiet waters of friendship. Like emotional acupuncturists, we know just where to put the needle. And do.

But we are each other's family. . . . I came late to the discovery that we would be related by marriage. I once made a fool of myself in front of a friend in the emergency room . . . after my husband's stomach and a bad fried clam had had an unfortunate meeting. "Are either of you related to him?" the nurse asked, and we both shook our heads until our friend prodded me gently in the side. "Oh, well, I'm his wife," I said. There's something so settled and stodgy about turning a great romance into next of kin on an emergency room form, and something so soothing and special, too. I suppose that is what I find so dreadful about divorce; lovers are supposed to leave you in the lurch, but your family is supposed to stick by you forever. "You can pick your friends, but you can't pick your relations," the folksy folks always say. Ah, but in this one case you can. You just don't realize it at the time.

Of course, what has happened is that I know the difference now between dedication and infatuation. . . . That doesn't mean I don't still get an enormous kick out of infatuation: the exciting ephemera, the punch in the stomach, the adrenaline to the heart. At a cocktail party the other night I looked across a crowded room and was taken by a stranger, in half profile . . . with a halo of backlighted curls. . . . And then he turned and I realized that it was the stranger I am married to, the beneficiary on my insurance policy, the sport jacket, the love of my life.

— Anna Quindlen,
from *Living Out Loud*

There are years that ask questions, and years that answer.

— Zora Neale Hurston,
quoted in *Simple Abundance*

Marriage is often described as a partnership; but it is a partnership which dissolves over the course of time into a sense of unity and mutuality unlike anything else known to humanity. It is not merely the passage of time. In our own days, we have recognized that it is at least as easy for a marriage to break up as to survive. So when we congratulate a couple on their wedding anniversary, we are hailing something far more happy and far more significant than mere survival. We are recognizing a very positive and triumphant achievement.

One reason the celebration of a wedding anniversary by friends and relatives is so joyous an occasion is that it shows the rest of us that lasting happiness is indeed attainable, and that it does indeed become the good fortune of some very nice people. . . .

A marriage is like an individual . . . It starts off very young, then grows into maturity, and gains in wisdom, in understanding. If it is a healthy marriage, it gets better with age. . . . in the traditional wedding service the participants are asked whether they "take" each other as lawful wedded wife and husband. I submit that the taking is far less important than the giving. But they have given, and continue to give, each other the real happiness.

— Leonard and Thelma Spinrad, *Speakers Lifetime Library*, "The Special Occasion Book"

Love seems the swiftest, but it is the slowest of all growths. No man or woman really knows what perfect love is until they have been married a quarter of a century.

— Mark Twain

I would like to have engraved inside every wedding band *be kind to one another.* This is the Golden Rule of marriage and the secret of making love last through the years.

— Randolph Ray

Happiness comes only when we push our brains and hearts to the farthest reaches of which we are capable.

— Leo Rosten

And we shall walk
through all our days
with love remembered and love renewed.

— Robert Saxton

"Love Is" List for a Gusto Husband

Some women married sentimentality. Every Valentine's Day these women get a $1.50 card at their plate with a heart on it and a present expensive enough to be called in on the charge card. I married gusto. At the birth of our first child, my husband leaned over, punched me on the arm and said, "Way to go, kid."

If you're going to live with gusto, you have to look for the little expressions of love that come each day. The following is a Valentine's Day [or I submit an Anniversary] message for such a man. If you are a gusto husband, clip it out, mount it on a lacy doily and kiss your wife when you give it to her. . . .

"LOVE"

Love is climbing out of a warm bed at night and checking to see if all the doors are locked when you think you hear something.

Love is giving you the pizza with two slices of pepperoni on it when I love pepperoni.

Love is acting excited over a $72 needlepoint canvas you bought when we both know you haven't finished the quilt, the pillow top, the kitchen curtains and the latch-hook rug.

Love is being mad at the kids at the same time you're mad at them.

Love is moving the car seat up as far as it will go when I get out, so you don't have to do it.

Love is painting a room together and letting you have the roller once in a while while I do the windowpanes.

Love is never remembering what birthday you're celebrating.

Love is learning how to make coffee and where the cups are.

Love is pretending to be jealous of your old boyfriend who became a priest.

Love is never going on a diet when you're fat.

Love is giving you the women's section of the paper to read first when the sports news is in the same section.

Love is refraining from telling you how the thermostat works.

Love is a lot of little things that add up to caring. It doesn't always add up to three little words. Sometimes, it adds up to six: I got your tank filled today.

— Erma Bombeck, *Forever, Erma*

The life of a Christian couple
has its own hidden heroism,
extraordinary heroism, in cruelly tragic
situations
that the world does not know of,
daily heroism in the unfolding succession
of sacrifices renewed at every hour.

There must be born in you
and grow ever stronger
the resolute desire
to be saints,
to be saints as husbands and wives,
in the marriage union itself,
in the very expression of your love.
— St. Augustine, *De Sancta Virginitate, PL 40, 424
and De Bono Vidvitatis, c 15, PL 40, 442* (respectively)
as cited by Joseph E. Kerns, S.J.,
in *The Theology of Marriage*

Love doesn't just sit there, like a stone, it has to
be made, like bread; re-made all the time, made
new.
— Ursula K. Le Guin, *The Lathe of Heaven*

Chapter 11.

Golden Marriages

Thoughts on What Makes a Marriage Work
from Couples Married 50 Years* or So

Always put God first. Always put God first.
So many times, we live through each other's
eyes, thinking our spouse knows better than we
do about how to make an important decision.
But the truth is, God knows more — God
knows how *He* wants us to make a decision. It
is important to take time to sit down and talk,
to do it in love, and to always invite Jesus in to
be present when you talk. We always say a
prayer together at night. And when we first got
married, the priest told us that no matter what
has gone on that day, to always kiss each other
good night. We have always — for nearly fifty
years — kissed each other good night.

> — Anonymous (Married forty-four years;
> four children; eight grandchildren)

---

*In some cases, couples married nearly fifty years were
interviewed. They were selected because of their devotion to the Catholic Church and their devotion to each
other.*

It is important to pray together daily. My husband is now eighty-seven, and I am eighty-five — we've been married fifty-seven years — I love every hair on his head . . . he's such a good man. . . . My advice to young people is to faithfully and loyally go to Mass. We have found married love to be very natural . . . the longer you live together, the more deeply you fall in love. You have to make sacrifices for each other and commit your life to a strong religion. Every night we kneel down together and pray six decades of the rosary — one for each of our children, and one for each other.

> — Anonymous (Married fifty-eight years;
> six children; fifteen grandchildren)

Marriage is permanent — like God's everlasting love. When we think of marriage, we think of "permanence," much like God's everlasting love. We went into marriage with the knowledge that this was a permanent thing — permanent — for better or for worse. We never thought, "Well, if this doesn't work out, or if you get sick, or if I meet someone else, we'll get divorced."

> — Anonymous (Married forty-two years;
> five children; three grandchildren)

Marriage is a triangular relationship. My husband and I believe that three of us walked down the isle the day we got married: my husband, myself, and Jesus. It is a triangular marriage, in which Christ is the head. Too often, I think, a bride and groom see marriage as a duo rather than a trio, and they don't include Christ. We believe the three become one. . . . Jesus has been ever present in our lives and has kept our marriage together. Jesus has always been there, prodding one or the other of us when we needed prodding. With Jesus' help we have always been able to work things out.

— Anonymous (Married forty-two years; four children, one foster child; eight grandchildren)

Friendship, fidelity, fun. We have what we call our "Three F's." Number 1 is fidelity — fidelity to God and fidelity to each other. Number 2 is friendship. We have to be friends to each other as well as to our other numerous friends. Number 3 is fun. It is important to have fun with each other, and to have fun with family and friends. And that is what we feel has sustained us.

— Anonymous (Married forty-eight years; eight children; twenty-one grandchildren)

Our Faith eliminated the gray areas. We believe in commitment and have raised our children to understand that marriage is a working proposition — it doesn't just happen by itself — just as you're always being re-credentialed with your job, taking workshops and courses to better yourself in your profession — you need to do that with your faith and your marriage. We went into marriage thinking it was for life. We've taught our children since they were very young that whenever they attempt to try something — once they've made a commitment to a team — they must complete the cycle. They can't say, "Well I'm tired of practice, so I'm not going anymore," or "I'm bored with this so I'm going to stop" . . . they weren't permitted to do that because our feeling was that until the season was over, you had made a commitment — the coach or teacher was counting on you, your teammates were counting on you — so you must complete the commitment. I think we are such a society now and I see it in schools, that "Johnny doesn't like a teacher," so the parents come in and request a change; kids in college "don't like a class," so they drop it; they "don't like a college," so they change schools. That transfers over to marriage, and the attitude is prevalent that "well, if we don't like this, we can get a divorce" kind of attitude — so we think that's a lot of what you are taught about commitments and contracts.

We believe there are many of benefits and graces of a Catholic marriage. We feel strongly that one of the main benefits or graces of a Catholic marriage is that there are simply no gray areas — we share the same views on abortion, we agree that there are to be no relationships before marriage, and we agree that there are to be no relationships outside of marriage. In short, we're made of the same sock.

— Anonymous (Married thirty-three years;
two children)

Marriage is more than saying "I Do." A Catholic marriage is more than saying "I do." It is a commitment that we made forty-six years ago — not only to each other, but to the third Participant, which is the Holy Spirit. The first book we bought for our marriage in 1953 was *Three to Get Married,* by Bishop Fulton J. Sheen, 1951. Our view of the Catholic religion is that it provides a foundation for our married life, with all of our commitment to each other, to the Ten Commandments, to the Sacraments, and to the Holy Spirit. Our commitment in the Sacrament of marriage is that we *do* make an effort to attend Mass as a couple and as a family when the children lived at home.

— Anonymous (Married forty-six years; five children; six grandchildren)

We weathered the storms of life. When I was very young and anticipating marriage, I could never have imagined that marriage would complete me so — bring me closer to my Creator and help me grow beyond my wildest dreams. For thirty-five years of loving fidelity, Christ took on a large dimension in our lives. We truly placed ourselves in His loving hands and were never disappointed. We raised nine children with His help, knew joys one could only imagine, and weathered the storms of life with the assurance that he would see us through. My husband, to me, was truly "Heaven Sent" — God's emissary in my life. God only *lent* him to me for thirty-five years, but what great years they were.

— Anonymous (Married thirty-five years; widowed; nine children; fourteen grandchildren)

Divorce is not in our vocabulary. Plain and simple — divorce is not in our vocabulary. Through difficult times of caring for ill relatives, ill parents, family deaths, and the complexities of raising children, we have always tried to do what we felt God wanted us to do. Catholicism has been the main ingredient. In recent years, we've been intensely studying the Bible and Apologetics. On Sunday, we're given Epistles and the Gospel; in addition, we have found that through daily meditations on the Gospels and other readings . . . Paul, Genesis, Deuteronomy . . . it is crystal clear through repetition and admonition that it is our *responsibility* to teach *our* children and *their* children the Ten Commandments. Daily reading and meditation has made us better Catholics. There is, in short, no question about it — marriage is not a contract; marriage is not two sharing a bed — but the two actually become one. That is why divorce is like losing a part of you. We are thankful to the Church for maintaining its integrity over the last 2,000 years.

— Anonymous (Married twenty-six years; four children; four grandchildren)

The Eucharist is central to our marriage. The Eucharist is central. I came to understand that primarily because my husband was not Catholic when we married, and only later did he convert to Catholicism. A benchmark in our lives was when we could share in the Eucharist together. The Eucharist is the outward sign given by Christ to show His grace. It is symbolic of the conjugal union. When my husband was not able to share in that, he was not a full witness. Once he converted — and after many years of marriage — in looking back we now realize that the Eucharist had become to us reconciling and nurturing . . . all that marriage had become.

— Anonymous (Married thirty-six years; two children; two grandchildren)

Catholicism has taken us on life's journey. Our mutual Catholic faith has been the bedrock of our marriage. From the initial vows of fidelity, love, and honor taken on the altar at our wedding Mass, we knew what was expected of each other and that we would need to function as "one" if we were going to succeed through the years of life's joys, trials, sorrows, and setbacks. We made these promises in *God's* house, and we knew we had to keep them to the very best of our ability.

Our Catholic faith is always there to guide us, to console us, and — yes — to reprimand us. It provides the road map to life's challenges, instructing us to love, honor, and serve the Lord. This takes good works, sacrifice, and prayer.

— Anonymous (Married forty-one years; three children; one grandchild)

Keeping things in context. Catholicism provides us with a common basis for working through problems and issues. It helps keep problems in context so we can better deal with them. Catholicism has given importance to our marriage and has sustained our marriage. Our strong commitment to Catholicism has given us the faith to deal with problems and work through them together.

— Anonymous (Married twenty-six years; six children; five grandchildren)

Our lives are centered in the Church. Our lives are "centered" in the Church. We share the same values . . . we have the same outlook. We have a common basis from which to work. And we do more *together* because we are active in the Church: we are Eucharistic ministers; Friendly Visitors; lecterns, Cursillistas [Cursillo is a fortifying "Course in Christ" whereby one then becomes a Cursillista — one who sees "the face of Christ" in others], and we attend daily Mass. We also have a priest in the family — one of our sons — and that is truly wonderful, not only because he has married all of our children and baptized all of our grandchildren, but also because we can go to him to receive clarification on new issues that arise in the Catholic Church. We are interested in keeping abreast of all developments in the Catholic Church so we can participate in our faith to the fullest. We sent all of our children to Catholic grade and high schools. Our lives — and now theirs — revolve around the Church.

— Anonymous (Married forty-five years;
seven children; seven grandchildren)

Raising our family as Catholics is our most basic value. Catholicism has been the basis of our marriage since we were dating. We've always believed that the family that prays together stays together. We pray together every night; we say grace before and after meals. We always try to go to Mass as a family, to have brunch afterwards, and to spend the rest of Sunday doing a family activity. It's so easy when the kids are little to split up and go scrambling in different directions. But we have always believed that it is important to stay together as a family — to go to Mass as a family.

—Anonymous (Married thirty years; three children)

Marriage is a Sacrament intended for life. Our belief has always been that God's plan for married people is what we should follow. We believe in the teachings of the Church — that marriage is a Sacrament and is intended to last for a lifetime — and that we receive the benefits of the sacramental life throughout our lives. Our faith has been *the* most important fact of our lives and our marriage. Because of our faith, we were always open to the gifts of new life and were able to welcome all of the seven children that God saw fit to sent us. One great honor of our lives has been the priestly vocation of our youngest son. Not all of our children are currently practicing their faith, but we are ever hopeful that in God's own time, they will return to the Church. One of the tenets of our faith is that we not become discouraged and lose hope when things don't go as we planned, but we accept that God's will, not ours, be done.

— Anonymous (Married forty-seven years;
seven children; six grandchildren)

Put God first. We met forty-nine years ago through a Catholic chaplain. We both used to go to daily Mass and the chaplain wanted us to meet because we had so much in common. We met, and six months later, married. God was — and still is — first in both of our lives. I was twenty-three and my husband traveled with the Air Force. I longed for him to be there with me to help make decisions, and sometimes I'd think, *I just can't do this.* And I'd call my mother and she'd say "now who's in charge here? You do all you can to make the right decision, but after you've done that, you put your head down on that pillow at night — and you put your heart in God's hands." I've always remembered that. We are much older now. We've lost two of our children, I had two miscarriages, and my husband is undergoing chemotherapy. I'm no longer without him when it comes to decision-making; but we still put our hearts in God's hands and let Him make the final decisions. I still remember what my mother said forty-nine years ago, and now *I* always say, "When you've done your best, you simply have to turn it over to God." I mean, how can anything go *wrong* with God in charge?

— Anonymous (Married forty-nine years; six pregnancies; four children; seven grandchildren)

Don't shy away from responsibility. We have always believed that it is important to have religion, faith in God, and faith in the Catholic Church — that is really the linchpin on why you don't decide to divorce. You have a *job* to make it work. Of course you will have difficulties and disagreements because we are human, and we have our faults. You have to accept these differences, and they will pass. You have to be definitely in love — not just physically — but with your spouse's character and qualities. As you encounter life's problems, it requires a spouse who doesn't shy away from these responsibilities. You have to take one step at a time . . . one day at a time. And you definitely have to have a sense of humor. I did not win my wife with my looks, but with my jokes.

— Anonymous (Married fifty-seven years; five children; ten grandchildren; two great grandchildren)

We give 100 percent to each other. Honesty is a big thing. We really feel O.K. with one another — we never feel like one or the other is hiding something or not telling us something, or not being honest. We have developed a real trust between the two of us. We both feel we give 100 percent to each other — it's not a 50/50 relationship. Even though our interests are very different, we still have a compatibility and a solid respect for each other's interests. Our faith is the main thing that has kept us together, and our love, and our interest in our children. And we never put each other down.

— Anonymous (Married thirty-six years; four children)

Our Faith provided us with a continuity. When we got married there was a kind of philosophy in the Catholic Church that the union of two people was seen as more than an expression of individual, shared love — it was also the responsibility of two married people to help each other fulfill their personal vocations of sainthood. And with the arrival of children, you were also expected to set them on the path to Heaven. So there was a social aspect to marriage, expressed in very strong terms that personal love was part of a larger meaning — a part of a relationship to a loving God — and that the love God had for us and we had for him was supposed to be passed on. And that gave us a communal or familial aspect, which made for a much stronger kind of family orientation in general. This idea of being "partners with God" was very strong . . . it resonated with me and my husband and has really been an important component of our marriage. Our personal faith and our religion provided our marriage with a kind of pathway . . . a continuity . . . one thing leading to another and, in a way, I think, *a protection* of our commitment by having this wider, shared interest and shared motivation for life. It placed marriage in a wider context, in a wider, bigger picture.

— Anonymous (Married fifty-one years; three children; one grandchild)

Teachings of the Church have provided blueprint. We are firm believers in the teachings of the Catholic Church. We respect what the Church teaches of marriage and the durability of marriage, how to live a proper life, and those activities that are to be avoided as expounded by the Catholic Church. The teachings of the Catholic Church have provided a blueprint, a pattern for how we have lived our lives together. The Church has been a strong and steady support of our lives through good times and bad. It has been a place of renewal, and we deeply value our activities with the Catholic Church. As Catholics, living our faith means all the same things as having a good marriage . . . in other words, you cannot have a good marriage without following the teaching of the Church, and you cannot follow the teachings of the Church and not have a good marriage. If we live our faith, our marriage will be solid and lasting.

— Anonymous (Married sixty years; three children; eleven grandchildren; ten great grandchildren)

Our children are saints in heaven. We've been married thirty-nine years; we have four living children and seven grandchildren. We lost two little girls at birth, early in our marriage. The severe personal pain and heartache that followed at the time of their death has now mellowed, and only a loving scar remains. Our two daughters, baptized at birth, now forever enjoy the Beatific Vision. How wonderful it is to know that two of our family are now saints in Heaven. Our Catholic faith is the blessed and firm foundation on which our marriage was built and with God's grace, the Blessed Mother's help, and the indwelling of the Holy Spirit, it continues to grow. Scripture says, "Do not despise little things." Throughout our marriage we have striven to do little things well toward each other and our children, whether it be a soft word, a loving glance, or a sweet smile. Such acts, which are the promptings of the Holy Spirit (1 Cor 12:1-12) make up the mortise of love. Our hope is that God's law of love revealed to us through His One, Holy, Universal, and Catholic Church and so lived, will at the end of our earthly pilgrimage unite us forever with our heavenly family.

— Anonymous (Married thirty-nine years; six children [two in heaven]; seven grandchildren)

Catholicism gives us a deep sense of important, shared values. One of the things we feel has played an important role in our marriage is that Catholicism has given us a deep sense of important, shared values, such as our dealings with children, the types of friends we share, our moral values, and our spiritual values. We both agree, too, that it isn't really necessary that two people in a marriage be of the same denomination, but the fact that we *do* share the same faith has made it easier — our relationship has come together in that way — in rearing children, approaching decisions, etc. — it makes it easier all the way around because you have the same values. Honesty is, of course, important, and that involves a willingness to say what we *really* feel even if it might be something uncomfortable. And equally important is taking the time to share our positive feelings with each other, too — that's always nice. We've enjoyed the blessing of good health, and of healthy children. We've learned a lot from our children about who we are. We've discovered that if you *really* listen to and *hear* your children, it helps you to know who you are. We are always trying to learn more about our faith through spiritual-growth programs and marriage-enrichment programs — those kinds of things have been invaluable. And our mutual sharing in the religious community has really helped us to grow together.

— Anonymous (Married forty-two years;
six children; four grandchildren)

You have to make big compromises. We both came from different backgrounds. I came from a close family with an open door — people were in all the time. My husband's family was much more introverted. The biggest thing we've learned over the years is that you have to make big compromises. We didn't have much, but my husband, who wasn't Catholic at the time, supported me fully in my faith, and it was his decision that the children go to Catholic school. So we made sacrifices. We lived on one small income so I could be home with the children. Today, people start out with two incomes and then live up to that, so it becomes very difficult to cut back to one. Another important thing for both of us is that we wanted our children to know their grandparents on both sides of the family, so they would have a sense of family and extended family. We didn't have family vacations like people do now. When we could get away, we used that time to visit family.

— Anonymous (Married fifty years; five children; four grandchildren)

Each of us is committed to the highest good. Our Catholic faith is the context for how we live our lives, how we address our problems, how we guide our children. It gives us a common basis for making both our everyday and our more difficult decisions. Each of us is confident that the other is committed to the highest good — namely Jesus and His Church. We also find support for our faith and marriage as we participate in the Mass, the Sacraments, and numerous other parish activities.

— Anonymous (Married thirty-one years; five children)

Our faith has been a comfort and consolation. We were married quite young. The first year of marriage was very difficult, but due to the Church and my belief in my religion and my commitment to the vows I took, I knew we should work through our differences. We've had our ups and downs over fifty-one years, but my faith has carried me, and I'm still here with the wife I love and cherish. We do a lot in terms of religious education, Bible studies, and furthering our religious education. We take advantage of the Sacrament of Reconciliation once a month and feel that it's a particularly special gift of the Catholic Church. If I were to give advice to people getting married today, I would encourage them to base their marriage on a strong faith in God because it is such an adhesive . . . it's the glue that holds people together. And if you don't share common beliefs and common values, it can be a disaster . . . I think our times show that.

— Anonymous (Married fifty-one years; five children; four grandchildren)

What God hath joined, let no man tear asunder. Catholicism played a major part in molding our marriage. We had been taught, and I strongly believed, that "What God hath joined together, let no man tear asunder." Each of us thought, too, that it was important that we chose a partner with a sense of humor — which has meant my wife has put up with my lousy puns for over fifty-four years, bless her heart.

— Anonymous (Married fifty-four years;
two children; three grandchildren)

Our love and mutual respect have grown over the years. It seems difficult to attempt to annunciate one's true feeling and recognition of a full and interesting life that has brought us to these blessed years in our marriage. We are both elderly, and we have had so much to live for over these joyful years that we try to stop daily in our full and busy lives to give thanks for our good fortune and for simply still being together. As we took our weddimg vows many years ago, we recognized that we had much in common as well as some areas of mutual concern that we had to consider when we repeated at Holy Mass those sacred vows "for better or for worse." Some of our areas of mutual concern included personal differences, but these were soon diminished as our love and respect for each other grew over the passing years. Some of these differences become more noticeable in retirement. There was no question that we had our differences and it was not uncommon that one of us may wish to spend more time watching something special on television, reading the sports column or editorials, or spending more time in the kitchen than seemed needed. As we became more tolerant of each other's likes and dislikes, however, we also became more involved in common interests and volunteering our time. We attempt to attend daily Mass, to pray the Rosary and to attend special novenas. At this point in our lives, we ask God and ourselves why are we here and what is our mission. We would like to be more helpful to our family, neighbors, and friends as we celebrate our sixtieth wedding anniversary. We feel, above all, that we are greatly, greatly blessed.

— Anonymous (Married sixty years; nine children; sixteen grandchildren)

Chapter 12.

AGING TOGETHER

Grow old along with me!
The best is yet to be,
The last of life, for which the first was made.
Our times are in His hand.
— Robert Browning, *Dramatis Personae,*
Rabbi Ben Ezra

Fifty years from now it will not matter what kind of car you drove, what kind of house you lived in, how much you had in your bank account, or what your clothes looked like. But the world may be a little better because you were important in the life of a child.
— Anonymous, *A 2nd Helping of*
Chicken Soup for the Soul

The worst of all tragedies is not to die young, but to live until I am seventy-five and yet have not ever truly to have lived [or loved].
— Martin Luther King, Jr.
in *A 2nd Helping of Chicken Soup for the Soul*

"What is REAL?" asked the Rabbit one day, when they were lying side by side near the nursery fender, before Nana came in to tidy the room. "Does it mean having things that buzz inside you, and a stick-out handle?" "Real isn't how you're made," said the Skin-Horse, "it's a thing that happens to you. When a child loves you for a long, long time, not just to play with, but REALLY loves you, then you become Real." "Does it hurt?" asked the Rabbit. "Sometimes," said the Skin-Horse, for he was always truthful. "When you are Real, you don't mind being hurt." "Does it happen all at once like being wound up," he asked, "or bit by bit?" "It doesn't happen all at once. You *become*. It takes a long time. That's why it doesn't often happen to people who break easily, or have sharp edges, or who have to be carefully kept. Generally, by the time you are Real most of your hair has been loved off, and your eyes drop out and you get loose in the joints and very shabby. But these things don't matter at all, because once you are Real, you can't be ugly, except to people who don't understand."

— Margery Williams, *The Velveteen Rabbit*

Believe Me,
If All Those Endearing Young Charms

Believe me, if all those endearing young charms,
Which I gaze on so fondly today,
Were to change by tomorrow,
and fleet in my arms,
Like fairy gifts fading away,
Thou wouldst still be adored,
as this moment thou art,
Let thy loveliness fade as it will,
And around the dear ruin each wish of my heart
Would intertwine itself verdantly still.

It is not while beauty and youth
are thine own,
And my cheeks unprofaned by a tear,
That the fervor and faith of a soul
can be known,
To which time will but make thee more dear;
No, the heart that has truly loved
never forgets,
But as truly loves on to the close,
As the sunflower turns on her god,
when he sets,
The same look which she turned when he rose.
— Thomas Moore, *Irish Melodies*, 1834

O God, you have taught me from my youth,
    and till the present I proclaim your wondrous
      deeds;
And now that I am old and gray,
    O God, forsake me not
Till I proclaim your strength
    to every generation that is to come.
Your power and your justice,
    O God, reach to heaven.
You have done great things;
    O God, who is like you?
Though you have made me feel many bitter
      afflictions,
you will again revive me;
from the depths of the earth you will once more
    raise me.
Renew your benefits toward me,
    and comfort me over and over.
So will I give you thanks with music on the lyre,
    for your faithfulness, O my God!
I will sing your praises with the harp,
    O Holy One of Israel!
My lips shall shout for joy
    as I sing your praises;
My soul also, which you have redeemed,
    and my tongue day by day shall discourse
      on your justice.

— Psalm 71:17-24,
The New American Bible

Come to me and I will give you rest
— all you who work so hard
beneath a heavy yoke —
Wear my yoke
— for it fits perfectly —
and let me teach you;
for I am gentle and humble,
and you shall find rest for your souls;
for I give you only light burdens.
— Matthew 11:28-30,
The Way, Complete Catholic Edition Bible

Meaning seems to come
with the passage of time.
— Patricia Livingston,
Lessons of the Heart

Youth longs and manhood strives,
but age remembers.
— Oliver Wendell Holmes,
The Iron Gate

The pastoral activity of the Church must help everyone to discover and to make good use of the role of the elderly within the civil and ecclesial community, in particular within the family.

In fact, the life of the aging helps to clarify a scale of human values; it shows the continuity of generations and marvelously demonstrates the interdependence of God's people.

The elderly often have the charism to bridge generation gaps before they are made: how many children have found understanding and love in the eyes and words and caresses of the aging!

And how many old people have willingly subscribed to the inspired word that the "crown of the aged is their children's children" (Prv 17:6)!

— Pope John Paul II, *Familiaris Consortio*

Perfect love sometimes does not come till the first grandchild.

— Welsh Proverb

Shall I compare thee to a summer's day?
Thou art more lovely and more temperate:
Rough winds do shake the darling buds of May,
And summer's lease hath all too short a date:
Sometimes too hot the eye of heaven shines,
And often is his gold complexion dimm'd,
And every fair from fair sometime declines,
By chance or nature's changing course
untrimm'd;
But thy eternal summer shall not fade
Nor lose possession of that fair thou ow'st,
Nor shall Death brag thou wander'st in his
shade,
When in eternal lines to time thou grow'st:
So long as men can breathe or eyes can see,
So long lives this, and this gives life to thee.

> — William Shakespeare, *Sonnets, XVIII*

Who well lives, for this age of ours
Should not be numbered
by years, days and hours.

> — Guillaume De Salluste,
> Seigneur Du Bartas, *Divine Weeks and Works*

For those who have not loved, old age is a wintertime of loneliness. The greatest human talent was buried in the ground so it would not be lost.

And in the end everything was lost. No one else came or cared. There was only a loveless person and a lonely waiting for death.

For those who have loved, old age is a harvest time. The seeds of love planted so carefully and so long ago have matured with time.

The loving person is surrounded in the twilight of life with the presence and the caring of others. The bread always comes back on the waters. What was given so freely and joyfully has been returned with interest.

— John Powell, S.J., *Happiness Is an Inside Job*

I remember the days of old; I meditate on all your doings, the works of your hands I ponder.

— Psalm 143:5, *The New American Bible*

On the other side of the nursery wall for all of us
there is our own old age,
the frailty, eccentricity, and wisdom
of our final time.

— Patricia Livingston, *Lessons of the Heart*

Memories are a Treasure
Memories are a treasure
time cannot take away . . .
So may you be surrounded
by happy ones today . . .
May all the love and tenderness
of golden years well spent
Come back today to fill your heart
with beauty and content.
— Helen Steiner Rice, *To Mother with Love*

What greater thing is there for two human souls,
than to feel that they are joined for life —
to strengthen each other in all labor,
to rest on each other in all sorrow,
to minister to each other in all pain,
to be one with each other in silent unspeak-
able memories at the moment of last parting?
— George Eliot, *Adam Bede*

It is love in old age,
no longer blind,
that is true love.
For love's highest intensity
doesn't necessarily mean
its highest quality.
Glamour and jealousy are gone;
and the ardent caress,
no longer needed,
is valueless
compared to the reassuring touch
of a trembling hand.
Passersby commonly see little beauty
in the embrace of young lovers
on a park bench,
but the understanding smile
of an old wife to her husband
is one of the loveliest things
in the world.

— Booth Tarkington
quoted in *Quiet Times for Couples*

To marry is to pledge to each other that you want
to grow old together.

— John F. Kippley, *Marriage Is for Keeps*

All the world's a stage,
And all the men and women merely players.
They have their exits and their entrances;
And one man in his time plays many parts,
His acts being seven ages. At first, the infant,
Mewling and puking in the nurse's arms.
And then whining schoolboy, with his satchel
And shining morning face, creeping like snail
unwillingly to school. And then the lover,
Sighing like furnace, with a woeful ballad
Made to his mistress' eyebrow. Then a soldier,
Full of strange oaths, and bearded like the pard,
Jealous in honour, sudden and quick in quarrel,
Seeking the bubble reputation
Even in the cannon's mouth. And then the justice,
In fair round belly with good capon lin'd,
With eyes severe and beard of formal cut,
Full of wise saws and modern instances;
And so he plays his part. The sixth age shifts
Into the lean and slipper'd pantaloon,
With spectacles on nose and pouch on side;
His youthful hose, well sav'd, a world too wide
For his shrunk shank; and his big manly voice,
Turning again towards childish treble, pipes
And whistles in his sound. Last scene of all,
That ends this strange eventful history,
Is second childishness, and mere oblivion,
Sans teeth, sans eyes, sans taste, sans everything."
— William Shakespeare,
As You Like It, Act II, Scene VII

Deep down we know that all is on loan to us.

Accidents happen, disease spreads, storms come, aging continues, jobs terminate, mistakes occur.

We go to bed one evening feeling good about life and ourselves. We awake in the morning and during the course of that day our world can be turned upside down by news of the death of a loved one, or an unexpected rift in friendship, or the loss of a priceless possession, or a doctor's prognosis, or an unexpected financial decision.

For the one who believes that all is on loan, this is to be expected.

Not that this expectation cripples the spirit of joy. Just the opposite is true; the present moment is treasured and enjoyed all the more because it is so precious and so fleeting. . . .

— Joyce Rupp, O.S.M., *Praying Our Goodbyes*

Chapter 13.

TILL DEATH DO US PART

Then sing, ye Birds, sing, sing a joyous song!
And let the young Lambs bound
As to the tabor's sound!
We in thought will join your throng,
Ye that pipe and ye that play,
Ye that through your hearts today
Feel the radiance which was once so bright
Be now for ever taken from my sight,
Though nothing can bring back the hour
Of splendour in the grass,
of glory in the flower;
We will grieve not, rather find
Strength in what remains behind;
In the primal sympathy
Which having been must ever be;
In the soothing thoughts that spring
Out of human suffering;
In the faith that looks through death,
In years that bring the philosophic mind.

— William Wordsworth,
Ode: Intimations of Immortality
from *Recollections of Early Childhood*

When you lay dying,
what it's about is the intimacy you've known,
the touch of another human being.
Ultimately,
what makes your life worthwhile
are the other people you've cared about.
— Sherry Lansing, *Cosmopolitan*, August, 1989

Death can be a bridge that leads the living to God as well as it leads those who have left us.

Our love wants to follow, our love refuses to let go.

Our hearts go crying after our dear ones . . . "Wait for me, wait for me!"

But they can't, they must continue their journey and we know we can't follow, not yet. We can only look up, earthbound.

And yet we sometimes feel their presence so powerfully there's no mistaking it.

And with it, the presence of God.
— Marjorie Holmes, *How Can I Find You God?*

To everything there is a season, and a time for every purpose under heaven.

> — Ecclesiastes 3:1,
> *King James Version Bible*

We must take our suffering and always view it from the perspective of the resurrection. We must look upon our goodbyes from the direction of hello. We must stand strong in the resurrection, believing that there is something beyond death, there is something beyond pain and hurt and heartache. Here is where our strength and hope lie. This is the power of the resurrection at work in us:

> "Do not grieve like those who have no hope. We believe that Jesus died and rose again, and that it will be the same for those who Have died in Jesus; God will bring them with him" (1 Thes 4: 13-14).
>
> — Joyce Rupp, O.S.M.,
> *Praying Our Goodbyes*

An Epitaph upon a Young Married Couple, Dead and Buried Together

To these, whom death again did wed,
This grave's their second marriage-bed.
For though the hand of fate could force
'Twixt soul and body a divorce,
It could not sunder man and wife
'Cause they both lived but one life.
Peace, good reader. Do not weep.
Peace, the lovers are asleep.
They, sweet turtles, folded lie
In the last knot love could tie.
And though they lie as they were dead,
Their pillow stone, their sheets of lead,
(Pillow hard, and sheets not warm)
Love made the bed; they'll take no harm;
Let them sleep, let them sleep on.
Till this stormy night be gone,
Till th' eternal morrow dawn;
Then the curtains will be drawn
And they wake into a light,
Whose day shall never die in night.

— Richard Crashaw (17th century),
The Norton Introduction to Literature: Poetry

Blessed are they who mourn,
for they will be comforted.
Blessed are those who hunger and thirst for
righteousness,
for they will be satisfied.
Blessed are those who are persecuted for the
sake of righteousness,
for theirs is the kingdom of heaven.

— Matthew 5:4, 6, 10,
The New American Bible

No one is without a family in this world:
the Church is a home and family for everyone,
especially those who "labor and are heavy
laden" (Mt 11:28).

—Pope John Paul II, *Familiaris Consortio*

Oh when I come to the end of my journey,
Weary of life, and the battle is won,
Carrying the staff and the cross of redemption,
He'll understand, and say "well done!"

— William Augustus Jones, Jr.

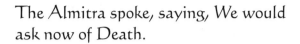

The Almitra spoke, saying, We would
ask now of Death.

And he said:
you would know the secret of death.

But how shall you find it unless you seek it
in the heart of life?

The owl whose night-bound eyes are blind
unto the day cannot unveil the mystery of light.

If you would indeed behold the spirit of death,
open your heart wide unto the body of life.

For life and death are one, even as the river
and the sea are one.

In the depth of your hopes and desires lies
your silent knowledge of the beyond;

And like seeds dreaming beneath the snow
your heart dreams of spring.

Trust the dreams, for in them is hidden the
gate to eternity.

Your fear of death is but the trembling of the
shepherd when he stands before the king whose
hand is to be laid upon him in honour.

Is the shepherd not joyful beneath his trembling, that he shall wear the mark of the king?

Yet is he not more mindful of his trembling?

For what is it to die but to stand naked in
the wind and to melt into the sun?

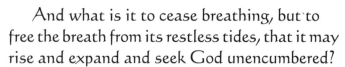

And what is it to cease breathing, but to free the breath from its restless tides, that it may rise and expand and seek God unencumbered?

Only when you drink from the river of silence shall you indeed sing.

And when you have reached the mountain top, then you shall begin to climb.

And when the earth shall claim your limbs, then shall you truly dance.

— Kahlil Gibran, *The Prophet*

God be in my hands and in my hearing.
God be in my head and in my understanding.
God be in my eyes and in my looking.
God be in my mouth and in my speaking.
God be in my heart and in my thinking.
God be at my end and my departing.

— Sarum Primer, in *Love in Action,* 1527

Jesus Christ stands for the Christian as the enduring sign of the promise of life through death.

— Evelyn Eaton Whitehead and
James D. Whitehead, *Marrying Well*

Two such as you with such a master speed
Cannot be parted nor be swept away
From one another once you are agreed
That life is only life forevermore
Together wing to wing and oar to oar.
— Robert Frost, *The Master Speed,* inscribed on the
gravestone of Frost and his wife, Elinor

Go from me. Yet I feel that I shall stand.
Henceforward in thy shadow. Nevermore
Alone upon the threshold of my door
Of individual life, I shall command
The uses of my soul, nor lift my hand
Serenely in the sunshine as before,
Without the sense of that which I forbore —
Thy touch upon the palm. The widest land
Doom takes to part us, leaves thy heart in mine
With pulses that beat double. What I do
And what I dream include thee, as the wine
Must taste of its grapes. And when I see
God for myself, He hears that name of thine,
And sees within my eyes the tears of two.
— Elizabeth Barrett Browning,
Sonnets from Portuguese, 6

Anyone is capable of going to Heaven.
Heaven is our home.
Dying is not the end, it is just the beginning.
Death is a continuation of life;
it is where our soul goes to God,
To be in the presence of God,
To see God,
To speak to God,
To continue loving Him with greater love.
We only surrender our body in death —
Our heart and soul live forever.

— Mother Teresa,
Meditations From A Simple Path

For I am convinced that neither
death, nor life,
nor angels, nor principalities,
nor present things, nor future things,
nor powers,
nor height, nor depth, nor any other creature
will be able to separate us
from the love of God
in Christ Jesus our Lord.

— Romans 8:38-39,
The New American Bible

Rest now, thou good and faithful servant.
Thou hast fought a good fight . . .
thou has finished the course . . .
thou hast kept the faith . . .
enter into the peace
of thy God everlasting.
— Elsie Robinson, in *Happy Marriage*

"The LORD gave and the LORD has taken away;
blessed be the name of the LORD!"

—Job 1:21,
The New American Bible

He will wipe away every tear from their
eyes, and there shall be no more death or
mourning, wailing or pain,
[for] the old order has passed away.

—Revelation 21:4,
The New American Bible

Do not be afraid.

— Jesus Christ

NOTES

Chapter 1: The Purpose of Marriage

Page 10. *The Way, Complete Catholic Edition, Including the Deuteroncanical Books* (Illinois: Tyndale House Publishers, and Indiana: Our Sunday Visitor Publishing, Inc., 1974).

Page 12. Dietrich Von Hildebrand, *Marriage: The Mystery of Faithful Love* (New Hampshire: Sophia Institute Press, 1984), p. xiii.

Page 13. Reverend George Anthony Kelly, *The Catholic Marriage Manual* (New York: Random House, Inc., 1958), p. 3.

Page 14. Drs. Evelyn and Paul Moschetta, *The Marriage Spirit* (New York: Simon and Schuster, 1998), p. 15.

Page 15. Bishop Fulton Sheen, *Three to Get Married* (New Jersey: Scepter, 1951), p. i. Reprinted with permission of the estate of Fulton J. Sheen.

Page 16. Reverend George E. Kelly, *The Catholic Marriage Manual,* p. 12.

Page 18. Michael G. Lawler, *Marriage and Sacrament* (Minnesota: Liturgical Press, 1993), p. 14. Published with permission of the Liturgical Press, Collegeville, MN.

Page 18. Dietrich Von Hildebrand, *Marriage: The Mystery of Faithful Love,* p. x.

Chapter 2: The First Year

Page 20. Frederick Saunders, *Salad for the Solitary and the Social, 1871,* as cited by Pat Ross, *I Thee Wed* (New York: Viking Studio Books, 1991), p. 8.

Page 21. Jon Nilson, *From This Day Forward* (Indiana: St. Meinrad Archabbey Press, 1983), pp. 16-17.

Page 22. Margaret Anderson, as cited in *A Woman's Notebook* (Pennsylvania: Courage Books, 1986), p. 76.

Page 22. Joseph Campbell as cited by Ellen Sue Stern, *Running on Empty* (New York: Bantam Books, 1992), p. 344.

Page 24. Bishop Fulton Sheen, *Three to Get Married,* p. 50.

Page 25. Jean Baptiste Lacordaire (1802-61), *Thoughts and Teachings of.*

Page 26. Harvey L. Ruben, M.D., *Supermarriage* (New York: Bantam Books, Inc., 1986), pp. 41- 42.

Page 28. Jon Nilson, *From This Day Forward,* p. 26.

Page 29. Martin G. Olsen Ed.D. and George Von Kaenel, S.J., *Two as One,* p. 102.

Page 30. Jean De Fabregues, *Christian Marriage* (New York: Hawthorn Books, 1959), pp. 20-21.

Page 31. Father John A. O'Brien, Ph.D., LL.D., *Happy Marriage: A Guide for Catholics* (Indiana: Our Sunday Visitor Press), p. 217.

Chapter 3: When the Sparks Stop Flying

Page 32. Bishop Fulton Sheen, *Three to Get Married,* p. 1.

Page 32. Martin G. Olsen Ed.D. and George Von Kaenel, S.J., *Two a One,* p. 83.

Page 33. Walter M. Abott, S.J., *The Church Today,* n. 49 as cited by John F. Kippley, *Marriage Is for Keeps* (Ohio: Foundation for the Family, 1994), p. 30.

Page 33. John F. Kippley, *Marriage Is for Keeps,* p. 47.

Page 34. Bishop Fulton Sheen, *Three to Get Married,* p. 51.

Page 36. John L. Thomas, S.J., *Beginning Your Marriage* (Buckley Publications, 1970), p. 71.

Page 37. Dietrich Von Hildebrand, p. 33.

Page 37. John L. Thomas, S.J., *Beginning Your Marriage,* p. 50.

Page 38. Jon Nilson, *From This Day Forward,* p. 45.

Page 39. M. Scott Peck, MD, *The Road Less Traveled* (New York: Simon and Schuster, Inc., 1978), pp. 84-85.

Page 40. Father A.H. Dolan, O. Carm., as cited by Father John A. O'Brien, *Happy Marriage,* p. 197.

Page 40. John L. Thomas, S.J., *Beginning Your Marriage,* p. 49.

Chapter 4: Walking the Journey

Page 43. Michael G. Lawler, *Marriage and Sacrament* (Minnesota: the Liturgical Press, 1993), p. 10.

Page 44. Hugh Prather, *For the Love of God,* "Walking Home" (California: New World Library, 1990), pp. 146-147.

Page 46. Dag Hammarskjold, *Markings,* as cited by Bernard Hayes, C.R., *Love in Action* (New York: Living Flame Press, 1985), p. 32.

Page 47. Edwin Muir as cited in Alanson B. Houghton, *Partners in Love* (New York: Walker and Company, 1988), p. ix.

Page 49. Dolores R. Leckey, *The Ordinary Way* (New York: Crossroad Publishing Co., 1982), p. 19.

Page 49. Denis De Rougement as cited by Harville Hendrix, Ph.D., *Getting the Love You Want* (New York: Harper and Row, 1988), p. 102.

Page 50. Bishop Fulton Sheen, *Three to Get Married*, p. 76.

Page 52. Jean De Fabregues, *Christian Marriage*, p. 1.

Chapter 5: Messages to a Wife

Page 55. *The Way, Complete Catholic Edition.*

Page 56. Father John Laux, M.A., *Catholic Morality* (Illinois: Tan Books and Publishers, Inc., 1990), p. 147.

Page 56. *The Jerusalem Bible* © 1966, 1967, 1968 by Darton, Longman, and Todd Ltd. and Doubleday, a Division of Bantam, Doubleday, Dell Publishing Group, Inc.

Page 57. H. Norman Wright, *Quiet Times for Couples* (Oregon: Harvest House Publishers, 1990), p. 14.

Page 58. *The Jerusalem Bible.*

Page 59. Anonymous as cited by Jack Canfield and Mark Hansen, *Chicken Soup for the Soul* (Florida: Health Communications, Inc.), p. 71.

Page 59. Albert Kirby Griffin, *Book of Religious Proverbs,* 1991.

Page 60. Edward Crowther, *Intimacy* (New York: Dell, 1986), p. 44.

Page 60. H. Norman Wright, *Quiet Times for Couples,* p. 36.

Page 60. Griffin, *Book of Religious Proverbs,* 1991.

Page 61. Michele Weiner-Davis, *Changing Her Man* (New York: Golden Books, 1998), p. 13.

Page 62. Anne Morrow Lindbergh as cited by H. Norman Wright, *Quiet Times for Couples,* p. 36.

Chapter 6: Messages to a Husband

Page 63-64. Father John O'Brien, *Happy Marriage*, p. 179.

Page 65. Alanson B. Houghton, *Partners in Love,* p. 19.

Page 66. Michael G. Lawler, *Marriage and Sacrament,* p. 23.

Page 66. Martin G. Olsen, Ed.D. and George Von Kaenel, S.J., *Two as One*, p. 83.

Page 67. *The Way, Complete Catholic Edition.*

Page 68. Father Thomas Keating, O.C.S.O., *Awakenings* as cited by James E. Adams, editor, *Living Faith* (Missouri: Creative Communications for the Church, 1997), reflection for March 19, 1997.

Page 70. *The New American Bible With Revised New Testament,* © 1986, 1970 by the Confraternity of Christian Doctrine, Washington, D.C. 20017. Used with permission.

Page 70. *Ibid.*

Page 71. *Ibid.*

Page 71. Griffin, *Book of Religious Proverbs*, 1991.

Page 73. Viscount Cowdray as cited by Father John A. O'Brien, *Happy Marriage*, p. 203.

Chapter 7: Encountering Life's Difficulties

Page 74. Peter Marshall as cited by Catherine Marshall, *The Best of Peter Marshall* (Michigan: Chosen Books, 1983), p. 336.

Page 74. William James as cited by Ellen Sue Stern, *Running on Empty,* p. 93.

Page 74. *The Way, Complete Catholic Edition.*

Page 75. Mother Teresa, *Meditations From A Simple Path* © 1996 by Mother Teresa. Reprinted by permission of Ballantine Books, a division of Random House Inc., p. 16.

Page 75. John Powell, S.J., *Unconditional Love* (Illinois: Argus Communications, 1978), p. 70.

Page 76. Dietrich Von Hildebrand, *Marriage: The Mystery of Faithful Love,* p. xi.

Page 76. Drs. Evelyn and Paul Moschetta, *The Marriage Spirit,* p. 181.

Page 77. Nisargadatta as cited by Dr. Evelyn and Paul Moschetta, *The Marriage Spirit,* p. 146.

Page 78. Robert Fulghum, *Handbook for the Soul*, p. 9.

Page 79. Father Benedict J. Groeschel, C.F.R., *Arise from Darkness* (California: Ignatius Press, 1995), p. 92.

Page 79. John L. Thomas, S.J., *Beginning Your Marriage,* p. 41.

Page 80. Patricia Livingston, *Lessons of the Heart* (Indiana: Ave Maria Press, 1985), p. 112.

Page 81. *Catechism of the Catholic Church, Prepared Following the Second Vatican Ecumenical Council* (New Jersey: Catholic Book Publishing, 1994), p. 427, n. 1718.

Page 82. Kathleen Norris, *After the Honeymoon — What?* as cited by Father John A. O'Brien, *Happy Marriage,* p. 201.

Page 83. *The New American Bible With Revised New Testament.*

Page 84. John De Fabregues, *Christian Marriage,* p. 61.

Page 85. Marjorie Holmes, *To Help You Through the Hurting* (New York: Doubleday, 1983), pp. 30-31.

Page 86. Jeanette and Robert Lauer, *Till Death Do Us Part* (New York: Hawthorn Press, 1988), p. 59.

Page 87. Cormac Burke, as cited by John Kippley, *Marriage Is for Keeps,* p. 32.

Page 88. Dolly Parton as cited by Cynthia and Robert Hicks, *The Feminine Journey: Understanding the Biblical Stages of a Woman's Life* (Colorado: NavPress, 1994), p. 133.

Chapter 8: Sharing in Life's Joys

Page 89. Mother Teresa, *Meditations From A Simple Path,* p. 87.

Page 90. Father John A. O'Brien, *Happy Marriage*, p. 79.

Page 91. Meister Eckhart, as cited by Ellen Sue Stern, *Running on Empty*, p. 40

Page 91. Nathaniel Cotton, *Rubicon Dictionary of Positive, Motivational, Life-Affirming and Inspirational Quotes*, compiled by John Cook (Connecticut: Rubicon Press, 1993), p. 43.

Page 92. Father John A. O'Brien, *Happy Marriage,* p. 161.

Page 93. *The New American Bible With Revised New Testament.*

Page 94. Henri J.M. Nouwen, *Lifesigns*, p. 103, (New York: Doubleday and Company, Inc., 1986), p. 103.

Page 94. Paul Tournier, quoted in *Peter's Quotations: Ideas for Our Time*, Laurence J. Peter, editor (Quill, 1993).

Page 95. Pope John Paul II, *Prayers and Devotions From John Paul II,* © 1984 by the K.S. Giniger Company Inc. Used by permission of Viking Penguin, a division of Penguin Putnam, Inc., p.60.

Page 96. Charles Morgan, *American Heritage Dictionary of American Quotes,* selected and annotated by Margaret Miner and Hugh Rawson (New York: Penguin), 1997.

Page 97. John Powell, S.J., *Happiness Is an Inside Job* (Texas: Tabor Publishing, 1976), p.106.

Page 97. C.S. Lewis, in *American Heritage Dictionary of American Quotes.*

Page 101. Bob Benson, *Laughter in the Walls* as cited by Bob Barnes, *Fifteen Minutes Alone With God (For Men)* (Oregon: Harvest House Publishers, 1995), pp. 141-143.

Chapter 9: Family Issues

Page 103. *The Way, Complete Catholic Edition.*

Page 103. "Motto" as cited by Father John A. O'Brien, *Happy Marriage*, p. 173.

Page 104. Peggy Noonan, "How Much Should a Parent Push?" *Good Housekeeping Magazine,* June 1998, p. 216.

Page 104. William Rankin Duryear's "Song for the Hearth and Home" as cited by Father John A. O'Brien, *Happy Marriage*, p. 203.

Page 105. *The Way, Complete Catholic Edition.*

Page 106. Dorothy Law Nolte and Rachel Harris, *Children Learn What They Live* (New York: Workman Publishing Co., 1998).

Page 107. Father John A. O' Brien, *Happy Marriage*, pp. 246-247.

Page 108. John F. Kippley, *Marriage Is for Keeps*, p. 41.

Page 108. Father John A. O'Brien, *Happy Marriage,* p. 69.

Page 108. Eric Fromm as cited by John Powell, S.J., *Unconditional Love* (Illinois: Argus Communications, 1978), p. 66.

Page 109. Michael Novak, *Family Out of Favor,* as cited by John Powell, S.J., in *Unconditional Love*, p. 93.

Page 109. Jacqueline Kennedy Onassis, *A Mother's Thoughts: A Journal of Notes and Quotes* (New York: Creations Ltd. in association with Red-Letter Press, Inc., 1994), p. 23.

Page 110. Rose Kennedy, *ibid.,* p. 57.

Page 110. *The New American Bible With Revised New Testament.*

Page 110. Erma Bombeck, *A Mother's Thoughts: A Journal of Notes and Quotes*, p. 75.

Page 111. Pope John Paul, from *Prayers and Devotions From John Paul II,* © 1984, p. 61.

Chapter 10: Happy Anniversary

Page 112. Kahlil Gibran as cited by Sue Ellen Stern, *Running on Empty,* p. 45.

Page 113. James Russell Lowell as cited by Sara Ban Breathnach, *Simple Abundance* (New York: Warner Books, 1955), June 23, entry.

Page 113. Jan and Myron Chartier, *Trusting Together in God* (Indiana: Abbey Press, Inc., 1984), p. 112.

Page 114. *Prayers for All Occasions* from the Basilica of the National Shrine of the Immaculate Conception, Washington, D.C., p. 69.

Page 115. Evelyn Eaton Whitehead and James D. Whitehead, *Marrying Well: Stages on the Journey of Chrisian Marriage* (New York: Image Books, 1983), p. 98. Reprinted with permission, © 1983, Whitehead Associates, 19120 Oakmont South, South Bend, IN 46637.

Page 116. Anna Quindlen, *Living Out Loud.* Copyright © by Anna Quindlen, reprinted by permission of Random House, Inc. pp. 74-75.

Page 118. Zora Neale Hurston as cited by Sara Ban Breathnach, *Simple Abundance,* January 1, entry.

Page 119. Leonard and Thelma Spinrad, *Speakers Lifetime Library*, "The Special Occasion Book" (New Jersey: Prentice Hall, 1979), p. 60.

Page 120. Mark Twain, quoted in *Peter's Quotations*.

Page 120. Randolph Ray, quoted in *Peter's Quotations*.

Page 120. Leo Rosten, *Rubicon Dicitonary of Postive, Motivational, Life-Affirming and Inspirational Quotes,* p. 43.

Page 120. Robert Saxton, *The Art of Robert Saxton,* "The Vow," in *Southern Living Magazine,* May 1999, p. 237.

Page 122. Erma Bombeck, *Forever Erma.* Copyright © 1996 by the estate of Erma Bombeck. Reprinted with permission of Andrews and McMeel Publishing. All rights reserved, pp. 193-194.

Page 123. St. Augustine, *De Sancta Virginitate, and De Bono Vidvitatis, as cited by* Joseph E. Kerns, S.J., *The Theology of Marriage* (New York: Sheed and Ward, 1964), p. 251.

Chapter 12: Aging Together

Page 146. Anonymous, as cited by: Jack Canfield and Mark Victor Hansen, *A 2nd Helping of Chicken Soup for the Soul* (Florida: Health Communications, Inc., 1995), p. 189.

Page 146. Martin Luther King, Jr. as cited by Jack Canfield and Mark Victor Hansen, *A 2nd Helping of Chicken Soup for the Soul,* p. 257.

Page 147. Marjorie Williams, *The Velveteen Rabbit* (New York: Avon Books, 1975), pp. 16-17.

Page 149. *The New American Bible With Revised New Testament.*

Page 150. *The Way, Complete Catholic Edition.*

Page 150. Patricia Livingston, *Lessons of the Heart,* p.13.

Page 153. John Powell, S.J., *Happiness Is an Inside Job,* p. 55.

Page 153. *The New American Bible With Revised New Testament.*

Page 153. Patricia Livingston, *Lessons of the Heart,* p. 16.

Page 154. Helen Steiner Rice, *To Mother with Love* (New York: Fleming H. Revell Company, 1991), p. 91.

Page 154. George Eliot, *Adam Bede* as cited by John Irving, *A Widow for One Year* (New York: Random House, 1998), pp. 402-403.

Page 155. John Kippley, *Marriage Is for Keeps,* p. 40.

Page 155. Booth Tarkington as cited by H. Norman Wright, *Quiet Times for Couples,* p. 27.

Page 157. Joyce Rupp, O.S.M., *Praying Our Goodbyes* (New York: Ivy Books, 1998 by Ave Maria Press), p. i.

Chapter 13: Till Death Do Us Part

Page 159. Marjorie Holmes, *How Can I Find You God?* (New York: Doubleday, 1975), pp. 30-31.

Page 160. Joyce Rupp, O.S.M., *Praying Our Goodbyes*, p. 49.

Page 161. Richard Crashaw, *An Epitaph Upon a Young Married Couple, Dead and Buried Together (1646)*. In *The Norton Introductin to Literature: Poetry,* edited by J. Paul Hunter (New York: W.W. Norton & Co., 1973), p. 345.

Page 162. *The New American Bible With Revised New Testament*.

Page 163. Kahlil Gibran, *The Prophet*, pp. 80-81.

Page 164. Evelyn Eaton Whitehead and James D. Whitehead, *Marrying Well*, p. 262.

Page 166. Mother Teresa, *Meditations From A Simple Path*, p. 50.

Page 166. *The New American Bible With Revised New Testament*.

Page 167. Elsie Robinson, as cited by Father John A. O'Brien, *Happy Marriage*, p 199.

Page 167. *The New American Bible With Revised New Testament*.

The following books that were used as resource materials:

The Book of Catholic Quotations, selected and edited by John Chapin (New York: Farrar, Straus, Cudahy, 1956).

The Columbia Dictionary of Quotations, Robert Andrews (New York: Columbia Press, 1993).

The Treasury of Religious and Spiritual Quotations: Words to Live By, Rebecca Davis and Susan Mesner (New York: The Reader's Digest Association, Inc., 1994).

John Bartlett's Familiar Quotes, 15th Edition (Canada: Little Brown and Co., 1980).

Speakers Lifetime Library, Leonard and Thelma Spinrad (New Jersey: Prentice Hall, 1979).

Our Sunday Visitor

Your Source for Discovering the Riches of the Catholic Faith

Our Sunday Visitor has an extensive line of materials for young children, teens, and adults. Our books, Bibles, booklets, CD-ROMs, audiocassettes, and videos are available in bookstores worldwide.

To receive a FREE full-line catalog, or for more information, call **Our Sunday Visitor** at **1-800-348-2440**. Or write: **Our Sunday Visitor**, 200 Noll Plaza, Huntington, IN 46750.

❑ Please send me a catalog.

Please send me material on:

❑ Apologetics/Catechetics   ❑ Reference works
❑ Prayer books   ❑ Heritage and the saints
❑ The family   ❑ The parish

Name _____

Address _____

City _____ ST _____ Zip _____

Telephone (_____) _____

AO3BBABP

❑ Please send a friend a catalog.

Please send a friend material on:

❑ Apologetics/Catechetics   ❑ Reference works
❑ Prayer books   ❑ Heritage and the saints
❑ The family   ❑ The parish

Name _____

Address _____

City _____ ST _____ Zip _____

Telephone (_____) _____

AO3BBABP

OUR SUNDAY VISITOR BOOKS

Our Sunday Visitor
200 Noll Plaza
Huntington, IN 46750
1-800-348-2440
E-mail us at: osvbooks@osv.com
Visit us on the Web: http://www.osv.com

Your source for discovering the riches of the Catholic Faith

You're Reading in the Wrong Direction!!

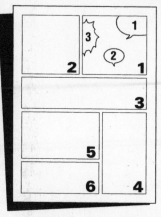

ALL ARE SIGNS OF MOMO'S SUPPOSED AFFECTION.

AAAHN

SKW

EEEZ

NIBBLING

SQUEEZING

PINCHING

PINCH

Whoops! Guess what? You're starting at the wrong end of the comic!

...It's true! In keeping with the original Japanese format, **Food Wars!** is meant to be read from right to left, starting in the upper-right corner.

Unlike English, which is read from left to right, Japanese is read from right to left, meaning that action, sound effects and word-balloon order are completely reversed... something which can make readers unfamiliar with Japanese feel pretty backwards themselves. For this reason, manga or Japanese comics published in the U.S. in English have sometimes been published "flopped"—that is, printed in exact reverse order, as though seen from the other side of a mirror.

By flopping pages, U.S. publishers can avoid confusing readers, but the compromise is not without its downside. For one thing, a character in a flopped manga series who once wore in the original Japanese version a T-shirt emblazoned with "M A Y" (as in "the merry month of") now wears one which reads "Y A M"! Additionally, many manga creators in Japan are themselves unhappy with the process, as some feel the mirror-imaging of their art skews their original intentions.

We are proud to bring you Yuto Tsukuda and Shun Saeki's **Food Wars!** in the original unflopped format.

For now, though, turn to the other side of the book and let the adventure begin...!

—Editor

BEGIN THE COUNTERATTACK! (END)

...AGAINST CENTRAL ROOKIE RENTARO KUSUNOKI!

...IS GOING TO BE THE CONQUEROR OF THE KITCHEN, RYO KUROKIBA...

AGAIN, YOU ONLY JUST FOUND OUT ABOUT THE CAPTAIN PART.

THAT'S A DIRECT ORDER FROM THE CAPTAIN OF THE CUTTING-EDGE COOKING RESEARCH SOCIETY, GOT IT?! AN ORDER!

GET 'IM, RYO! I FORBID YOU TO LOSE, YOU HEAR ME?!

BUT MOST OF ALL...

I SEE. SO THAT MEANS YOU GOT TARGETED BY CENTRAL'S MOP-UP TOO, HUH.

I WAS, LIKE, TOTES SURPRISED, YA KNOW?!

I THOUGHT I WAS JUST, LIKE, TAKING ALL THEIR STUFF...

OH MY GAWD!

Notice Of Shokugeki

Cutting-Edge Cooking Research Society

Captain: Alice Nakiri

...BUT SOMEHOW, WHEN THEY DID THE PAPERWORK, MY NAME GOT PUT DOWN AS THE NEW SOCIETY CAPTAIN!

YOU KNOW, I HAVE A NEW APPRECIATION FOR THE WORD "CAPTAIN."

DON'T YOU THINK IT HAS A BIT OF A RING TO IT? I TOTALLY WON'T MIND IF YOU ALL CALL ME "CAPTAIN ALICE" FROM NOW ON.

UH... YOU DIDN'T EVEN KNOW YOU WERE A CAPTAIN UNTIL A FEW DAYS AGO.

!

IT'S RYO WHO'S TAKING UP THE CHALLENGE.

OH NO, NOT ME.

THEN THIS MEANS WE GET A CHANCE TO WATCH YOU COOK FOR THE FIRST TIME IN A WHILE. AWESOME!

WHAT ARE THE TWO OF YOU DOING HERE?

YEP! OUR SHOKUGEKI IS UP NEXT!

DON'T TELL ME...

REALLY? I NEVER KNEW YOU WERE PART OF A RESEARCH SOCIETY.

I KNOW, RIGHT? I WAS *TOTALLY* SHOCKED TOO! SEE, IT'S A LONG STORY, BUT...

?

TWO YEARS AGO, WHEN I WAS IN MIDDLE SCHOOL, I CHALLENGED THE CAPTAIN OF THE CUTTING-EDGE COOKING RESEARCH SOCIETY TO A SHOKUGEKI.

I WON BY A LANDSLIDE, OF COURSE, WHICH MADE THEIR KITCHENS AND EQUIPMENT ALL MINE.

WINNER!!

WELL, THAT SEEMS EXCES-SIVE.

THOUGH I GUESS BOTH SIDES DID AGREE TO THOSE CONDI-TIONS.

LOSER

MR. OIZUMI.

I SEE THE BOTH OF YOU HAVE MATURED EVEN FURTHER SINCE I LAST SAW YOU IN THE FALL CLASSIC.

HEH HEH.

MURMUR

OH, SO HE'S GONNA BE DOING ANOTHER SHOKUGEKI RIGHT NOW?

MURMUR

R-REALLY?

YOUR WORDS A MOMENT AGO MADE THIS OLD MAN PROUD!

ESPECIALLY YOU, YOUNG ALDINI!

THE NEXT CHAL-LENGERS ARE TWO YOUNGSTERS YOU BOTH KNOW WELL.

HA HA HA!

...?

ER! B-BY THE WAY, MASTER OIZUMI, WHICH RESEARCH SOCIETY IS HAVING ITS SHOKUGEKI NEXT?

WHA ...?

HM?!

AH!

WHIRL

N A B

I THINK I'M GONNA CRUSH YOU BOTH RIGHT HERE, RIGHT—

BAD.

NO FIGHTING.

STOMP

STOMP

H-HEY! SHIGE!

FOR A SELF-PROCLAIMED ELITE, I'M FAILING TO SEE WHAT'S SO *ELITE* ABOUT YOU.

YOUR CONTINUAL EMPHASIS OF YOUR CHOSEN STATUS SOUNDS LESS LIKE A STATEMENT OF FACT AND MORE LIKE A DESPERATE DENIAL OF YOUR OWN INFERIORITY.

OH?

IN FACT, IT ALMOST SOUNDS LIKE YOU'RE CLINGING TO CENTRAL FOR THE SLIVER OF IDENTITY AND SELF-WORTH IT SEEMS TO GIVE YOU.

YEAH, SENPAI. WHAT *HE* SAID. WHAT DO YOU THINK OF *THAT?*

WHOA, TAKUMI! THAT WAS SOME SERIOUSLY DEEP STUFF!

...

THAT YOU FEEL THE NEED TO KEEP PRAISING YOURSELF WITH WORDS LIKE "ELITE" AND "SUPERSTAR"...

Y'KNOW, I WAS GONNA GO EASY ON YOU BECAUSE YOU'RE JUST A PAIR OF FIRST-YEARS...

HA HA...

...BUT TO HELL WITH THAT.

...TELLS ME THAT YOU HAVE LITTLE TO NO CONFIDENCE IN YOUR OWN ABILITIES.

OF COURSE! OF ALL THE STUDENTS IN THIS INSTITUTE, *I* WAS CHOSEN TO BE A FOUNDING MEMBER OF CENTRAL!

IN OTHER WORDS, I WAS HANDPICKED TO BE A LEADER—A *RULER* OF THE THOUSANDS OF STUDENTS AT TOTSUKI.

FAMILY-RESTAURANT CHEFS!

BA A A N

ESPECIALLY YOU TWO. YOU'RE LIKE THE COMMONEST OF THE COMMON.

WE WHO WERE CHOSEN BY CENTRAL ARE THE BEST! THAT MEANS ALL OF YOU ARE JUST THE REST!

SWF

OUT OF EVERYBODY HERE, THE DEAN OF THE TOTSUKI INSTITUTE, AZAMI NAKIRI HIMSELF, CHOSE US.

SO IF I WERE YOU, I WOULDN'T CAUSE TOO MUCH TROUBLE. YOU CATCH MY DRIFT?

THAT MAKES US THE ELITE! WE ARE SUPERSTARS, AND NO ONE CAN SAY OTHERWISE!

CENTRAL

178

RMBL RMBL RMBL RMBL RMBL RMBL

OH YEAH? SO CENTRAL, LIKE, WON *EVERYTHING* IN HALL C? AWESOME!

IT'S TOTALLY SMOOTH SAILING OVER HERE TOO!

NOTHING OUT OF THE ORDINARY AT ALL...

YO, DUDE! DON'T GET DISTRACTED WHEN YOU'RE TALKIN' TO ME!

OH, HEY, MR. OIZUMI! MR. SAOTOME! IT'S BEEN A WHILE!

AND TAKUMI ALDINI TOO!

WELL, IF IT ISN'T YOUNG YUKIHIRA!

PRETTY MUCH, YEAH.

WHAT, YOU DOWN HERE JUST TO SCOPE US OUT?

SO YOU'RE THE KID WHO BEAT EIZAN, EH? AND YOU. YOU WERE IN THE FALL CLASSIC SEMIFINALS, RIGHT?

FIFTH SEAT: SOMEI SAITO (THIRD-YEAR)
SIXTH SEAT: NENE KINOKUNI (SECOND-YEAR)
FORMER SEVENTH SEAT: SATOSHI ISSHIKI (SECOND-YEAR)
FORMER EIGHTH SEAT: TERUNORI KUGA (SECOND-YEAR)
NINTH SEAT: ETSUYA EIZAN (SECOND-YEAR)
TENTH SEAT: ERINA NAKIRI (FIRST-YEAR)

THAT WAS THE COUNCIL OF TEN'S SIXTH SEAT, NENE KINOKUNI.

SHE'S THE ONE WHO HOLDS THE HIGHEST SEAT ON THE COUNCIL AFTER THE THIRD-YEARS.

IT WOULDN'T BE A STRETCH TO SAY SHE STANDS A CUT ABOVE NOT JUST US BUT THE SECOND-YEARS TOO.

ENOUGH!

AND DON'T FORGET THE SPEEDO!

I-I DON'T KNOW WHAT THAT MEANS!

NOBODY CAN PULL OFF THE NAKED APRON AND LOINCLOTH LOOKS LIKE HE CAN!

HEY! WHATCHU TALKIN' ABOUT?! ISSHIKI SENPAI IS THE BEST OF THE SECOND-YEARS, HANDS DOWN!

WE'RE FINISHED HERE.

THIS IS KINOKUNI, IN HALL C.

HELLO, HELLO! THIS IS HALL D!

176

HALL C

CENTRAL HAS EMERGED VICTORIOUS IN ALL CONTESTS!

LADIES AND GENTLEMEN, THIS CONCLUDES TODAY'S SHOKUGEKI.

DID YOU RECORD ALL OF THAT?

YEAH. MAN, THAT WAS FREAKIN' INTENSE!

...

DOOM

154 BARING FANGS

YOU SAY SOMETHING, LITTLE FIRST-YEARS?

ON NO! I ONLY TOOK MY EYES OFF OF HIM FOR ONE SECOND!

YEAH. JUST THOUGHT YOU OUGHTA KNOW THAT WE DON'T RESPOND WELL...

TAKUMI TOO?!

...TO PEOPLE THINKING THEY CAN JUST ARBITRARILY DECIDE OUR WORTH!

BUT THAT MAKES IT SO MUCH MORE AWESOME WHEN WE WIN, MOMO SENPAI!

HMPH. HOW DISTASTEFUL, GOING OUT OF YOUR WAY TO INSULT THE OTHER GUYS LIKE THAT.

SCOFF AT US ALL YOU LIKE...

WE'VE MADE IT THIS FAR AT TOTSUKI OURSELVES, YOU KNOW.

WE WILL NOT HAND YOU AN EASY VICTORY!

Victoria
Spanish Cooking Resear

WE'RE ALL SOCIETIES THAT ALSO FINISHED IN THE TOP RANKS OF THE MOON FESTIVAL.

YEAH, IT'S FINE, IT'S FINE!

ARE YOU REALLY SURE THIS IS OKAY?

ER... ABOUT THE SHOKU-GEKI THEMES...

BUT LIKE WE SAID BEFORE, THIS ONE TIME WE'RE DOING YOU GUYS A FAVOR.

WHEN PICKING A THEME FOR A SHOKUGEKI, I KNOW THAT AGREEING ON SOMETHING THAT'S SOMEWHERE IN BETWEEN BOTH SIDES' FIELDS OF EXPERTISE IS NORMAL.

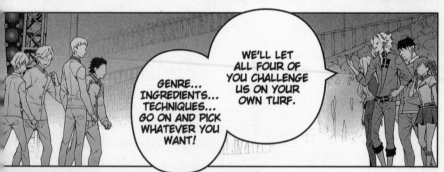

GENRE... INGREDIENTS... TECHNIQUES... GO ON AND PICK WHATEVER YOU WANT!

WE'LL LET ALL FOUR OF YOU CHALLENGE US ON YOUR OWN TURF.

...USING THOSE VERY TECHNIQUES YOU'VE TRIED OH SO HARD TO PERFECT.

WE DECIDED THAT IT'D BE WAY MORE FUN TO CRUSH YOU...

COME TO THINK OF IT, I HAVEN'T DONE MUCH IN THE WAY OF BAKING AND CONFECTIONS MYSELF.

HUH! TOTSUKI IS A SCHOOL KNOWN MOSTLY FOR MAIN DISHES AND STUFF, BUT SHE GOT ON TO THE COUNCIL FOR BEING GOOD AT DESSERTS?

WOW!

A CRUSHING VICTORY FOR CENTRAL IN BOTH CASES.

I KNOW... I KNOW...

YUKIHIRA! REMEMBER, WE ARE HERE **ONLY** TO OBSERVE AND RECONNOITER. NO CHALLENGING PEOPLE TO SHOKUGEKI WILLY-NILLY.

I WANNA CHALLENGE HER.

FLICKR FLICKR

DAMN IT!

FOR THE REST OF YOUR LIFE, I'M GOING TO MAKE YOU REGRET HUMILIATING ME!

WE AREN'T DONE, YUKIHIRA. NOT BY A LONG SHOT!

WHUMP

MRRRGH!

...HAVE WON THEIR CHALLENGES IN DOMINATING FASHION!

Central Western Food Research Society 0-3

Central Chocolate Research Society 0-3

160

DUN

GLITTER

GLITTER

WAAAAA

LADIES AND GENTLEMEN, BOTH MOMO AKANEGAKUBO AND ETSUYA EIZAN...

BUT WE MUST NOT LET OUR-SELVES BE OVER-WHELMED!

IT... IT'S BEAUTIFUL.

ALMOST BLIND-INGLY SO!

WE MUST JUDGE IT FOR ITS TASTE!

SHE RIPPED THE HANDS OFF HER OWN STUFFED ANIMAL TO USE THEM AS OVEN MITTS... NO MATTER HOW OFTEN I SEE THAT, IT STILL DISTURBS ME.

HMM... DID IT BAKE OKAY?

S I L E N C E

FOOMP

GASHAK

AND ME.

SHMP

SHMP

SHMP

JUDGING A DESSERT-THEMED SHOKUGEKI BRINGS BACK MEMORIES OF THAT ONE PARTICULAR FALL CLASSIC ROUND.

IT DOES.

OH GOOD. IT LOOKS RIGHT.

THE CHOCOLATE RESEARCH SOCIETY

RANKING FOURTH OVERALL IN PROFITS IN THE MAIN STREET AREA DURING THE MOON FESTIVAL, THEY ARE CONSIDERED ONE OF THE INSTITUTE'S POWERHOUSE SOCIETIES!

...ALL WITH THE INTENT OF USING THAT KNOWLEDGE TO FURTHER THEIR ART OF DESSERT MAKING!

AS A CLUB, THEY HAVE DEDICATED THEMSELVES TO THE RESEARCH OF THAT BASE INGREDIENT OF ALL CHOCOLATE-CACAO. THEY STUDY ALL ASPECTS OF THE BEAN-WHERE AND HOW IT IS GROWN, THE DIFFERENT VARIETIES, HOW TO FERMENT AND ROAST THEM...

I THINK IT'S ABOUT TIME THE CAKE LAYER HAS FINISHED BAKING...

YANK

SWFF

MAYBE THE BOWL SOCIETY DOES HAVE THEIR SHOKUGEKI TODAY.

AND I WONDER WHAT'S GOING ON WITH HAYAMA AND THE ISHIOMI SEMINAR HE'S A PART OF. THEN THERE'S ALSO KUGA SENPAI AND HIS CHINESE-FOOD RESEARCH SOCIETY.

...

RING

BIP BIP

I'VE BEEN TRYING TO GET AHOLD OF NIKUMI AND KONISHI THIS WHOLE TIME, BUT NEITHER IS PICKING UP.

TP TP TP

I KNOW, I KNOW! C'MON, LET'S GO!

BE SURE YOU CLOSELY WATCH THE OPPOSITION'S CHEFS AND WHAT THEY CAN DO!

YUKIHIRA! I'M SURE I DON'T NEED TO REMIND YOU, BUT WE'RE HERE ONLY FOR RECONNAIS-SANCE!

UM, IT LOOKS LIKE THEY'VE STARTED THE FIRST ROUND OF SHOKUGEKI ALREADY.

DOOM

Western Food Research Society vs Central

WHERE
ON EARTH
DID SHE
GET THAT
NAME?

MOMO SENPAI'S STUFFED ANIMAL
NAME: BUTCHY

148

HALL A
GROUP

HALL B
GROUP

HALL C
GROUP

SO I'M GONNA DO SOMETHING ABOUT IT. THAT'S ALL.

THAT WAS THEN, AND THIS IS NOW. AND RIGHT NOW...

...THERE'S STUFF GOING ON I'M NOT SURE I AGREE WITH.

...

YUKIHIRA! I'M SORRY I KEPT YOU WAITING.

WELL, SEE YA LATER, NAKIRI! TAKE CARE OF YOURSELF.

146

YUKIHIRA! WAIT RIGHT THERE. I'M GOING TO GO GET READY.

ALL RIGHT, I, UH...I'LL BE OFF, THEN.

QUAD STAR

RUSTLE

RUSTLE

DOESN'T IT BOTHER YOU AT ALL? WHAT AZAMI NAKIRI...

QUAD STAR

...?

YUKIHIRA.

A LOT OF SURPRISING STUFF HAPPENED THAT NIGHT, SURE.

WHAT MY FATHER SAID.

IS SHE STILL NOT FEELING ANY BETTER?

B-BUT I CAN'T LEAVE MISS ERINA ALONE IN HER, AH, PRESENT CONDITION...

RECONNAISSANCE?

SHE'S BEEN OUT OF IT SINCE THAT NIGHT NAKAMURA SENPAI STOPPED BY.

ARE YOU SURE, MISS ERINA?

HISAKO, I WILL STAY HERE AND REST. YOU GO ALONG AND HELP THE OTHERS WITH WHATEVER IT IS THEY ARE DOING.

I-I WILL BE PERFECTLY FINE, THANK YOU! I'M FEELING MUCH BETTER!

I-I CAN MANAGE THIS MUCH BY MYSELF, THANK YOU!

OH! AND HERE IS A CUP AND NAPKIN ...

I'LL LEAVE AN ELECTRIC KETTLE RIGHT HERE. AND THE MEDICINE WILL BE RIGHT HERE AS WELL.

OH! IF YOU FEEL DIZZY AGAIN, PLEASE TAKE THIS CHINESE REMEDY. WITH HOT WATER, IF POSSIBLE!

IF ANYTHING HAPPENS, PLEASE CALL ME ON MY CELL PHONE IMMEDIATELY!

IS ISSHIKI NOT HERE TODAY?

NOPE. HE TOOK OFF EARLIER, SAYING HE HAD ERRANDS TO RUN.

MAYBE WE COULD ASK MISS FUMIO.

WELL, IF YOU'RE ALL GONNA BE THAT WAY...

...THEN WE DON'T HAVE ANY CHOICE *BUT* TO HELP!

YEAH. IF YOU'RE GOING, BIG BRO, I'M GOING TOO.

YOU WILL?

YOU BET! NOW LET'S GET EVERY-BODY SPLIT INTO GROUPS!

OH YEAH! HANG ON A SEC, EVERYONE.

AFTER ALL, IT'S FAR TOO WORRISOME LETTING YOU WANDER OFF ON YOUR OWN, YUKIHIRA.

TAKUMI-CHI!

UM, I-I WANT TO GO TOO!

YES. AND IS IT ME, OR HAS TAKUMI PRACTICALLY MOVED INTO THE DORM ALREADY?

IF HE HAS TAKUMI-CHI WITH HIM, I GUESS HE'LL BE OKAY...

AWESOME! LET'S GO TAKUMI!!

IT MAY BE WISER IF WE SPLIT UP.

WHAT ABOUT YOU, MARUI? WANNA COME TOO?

RECON-NAISSANCE, HM? IN THAT CASE...

OOH, GOOD IDEA, TADOKORO! C'MON!

THAT WAY MAYBE I'LL GET TO WATCH THE PERSON WHO WILL BE ASSIGNED TO THE SHOKUGEKI AGAINST THE HOME COOKING SOCIETY!

! GLEAM

NOW I NEED TO SEE WHAT THEY'RE LIKE.

URK

GOOD JOB OPENING YOUR FAT MOUTH, MARUI.

THIS IS YOU WE'RE TALKING ABOUT! OF COURSE SOMETHING COULD GO WRONG!

NAAAH! IT'LL BE FINE! I MEAN, I'M JUST GONNA WATCH. WHAT COULD POSSIBLY GO WRONG?

I WONDER... IS THERE ANY WAY I COULD MAYBE SNEAK IN AND WATCH ONE OF THEIR SHOKUGEKI?

FLICKER

WHAT, THIS IS MY FAULT?!

WHOA, WHOA! ARE YOU SURE YOU SHOULD GO AROUND STICKING YOUR NOSE IN THINGS? WON'T YOU JUST GET IN MORE TROUBLE?

FLICKER   FLICKER

FINE. THEN I'M GOING WITH YOU.

...

Dean

Council of Ten

THE STUDENTS ALREADY SELECTED ARE EXCEPTIONALLY TALENTED. IN FACT, THEY'RE SO GOOD YOU COULD CALL THEM "THE COUNCIL RESERVE"!

General Student Body
(Azami Administration Sympathizers)

(Resistance)

...AND ONE BY ONE, THEY ARE ALL SIDING WITH THE AZAMI ADMINISTRATION!

EVERY ONE OF THEM HAS THE POTENTIAL TO SOMEDAY JOIN THE COUNCIL OF TEN...

CHEFS SO GOOD THEY'RE CALLED THE COUNCIL RESERVE...

CENTRAL, EH?

I'M SURE EVERY GROUP HAS TO BE ON PINS AND NEEDLES RIGHT NOW.

FOR BETTER OR WORSE, THE MIYAZATO SEMINAR THAT I ATTEND AND TADOKORO'S HOME COOKING SOCIETY BOTH HAVE THEIR SHOKUGEKI SCHEDULED FOR A LATER DATE.

TODAY CENTRAL BEGINS ITS MOP-UP OF THE RESISTANCE...

...WITH THE FIRST ROUND OF SHOKUGEKI CHALLENGES.

WOW. I DIDN'T KNOW CENTRAL WAS STILL SO SMALL.

HUH. OKAY.

THAT MEANS THEY'RE GOING TO SPLIT THE SHOKUGEKI UP INTO DIFFERENT GROUPS AND DO THEM SEPARATELY.

PRESENTLY THERE ARE ALMOST 100 SOCIETIES AND SEMINARS THAT HAVE YET TO OFFICIALLY FOLD.

WAIT, THIS IS JUST THE FIRST ROUND?

THERE'RE GOING TO BE MORE?

BUT CENTRAL ONLY HAS SOMETHING AROUND THIRTY MEMBERS, AND THAT INCLUDES THE COUNCIL OF TEN.

IF HE'S STILL IN THE SCREENING PROCESS, WE CAN EXPECT CENTRAL'S NUMBERS TO CONTINUE TO RISE.

FROM WHAT I'VE HEARD, AZAMI NAKIRI HIMSELF HANDPICKS ITS MEMBERS. IT'S PROBABLY GOING TO TAKE SOME TIME BEFORE HE FINDS EVERYBODY HE WANTS.

CONVERSELY, SHOULD THE PARTY OF THE SECOND BE DECLARED THE WINNER, THE PARTY OF THE FIRST IS REQUIRED TO SUBMIT TO THE ORDER BY THE AZAMI ADMINISTRATION TO DISBAND. NOTE: REFUSAL TO SUBMIT TO THE ORDER IN THIS CASE WILL RESULT IN EXPULSION.

THIRD ARTICLE (CONDITIONS FOR VICTORY). SHOULD THE PARTY OF THE FIRST BE DECLARED THE WINNER OF THE SHOKUGEKI, THEIR RESEARCH SOCIETY AND/OR SEMINAR WILL BE PERMITTED TO CONTINUE TO OPERATE AS NORMAL.

SECOND ARTICLE (SHOKUGEKI THEMES AND SCHEDULING). THE PARTY OF THE FIRST AND THE PARTY OF THE SECOND ARE REQUIRED TO MEET PRIOR TO THE SHOKUGEKI TO SETTLE UPON A THEME AND SCHEDULE AGREEABLE TO BOTH PARTIES.

YOU WILL NOTICE IN THE NEXT ARTICLE WHAT ISSHIKI INTENDED.

...? THESE SEEM NORMAL TO ME.

ONCE CHOSEN, IT IS FORBIDDEN FOR JUDGES TO COME INTO CONTACT WITH EITHER THE PARTY OF THE FIRST OR THE PARTY OF THE SECOND AT ANY TIME BEFORE THE OFFICIAL COMMENCEMENT OF THE SHOKUGEKI. NOTE: SHOULD THERE BE ANY CONTACT, THE SHOKUGEKI WILL IMMEDIATELY BE DECLARED INVALID AND A NEW ONE WITH NEW JUDGES WILL BE SCHEDULED FOR A LATER TIME.

AN ODD NUMBER OF MEMBERS FROM NATIONAL RESTAURANTS, CULINARY GROUPS AND/OR OTHER FOOD-RELATED BUSINESSES WILL BE SELECTED AT RANDOM AND ASSIGNED TO JUDGE A RANDOM SHOKUGEKI.

SHOKUGEKI JUDGES ARE TO BE NEUTRAL PARTIES UNAFFILIATED WITH EITHER THE PARTY OF THE FIRST OR THE PARTY OF THE SECOND AND NOT PRESENTLY CONNECTED WITH OR IN THE EMPLOY OF THE TOTSUKI INSTITUTE.

FOURTH ARTICLE (JUDGES AND JUDGING).

THAT WAS A SMART MOVE.

FAIR AND IMPARTIAL JUDGING IS PRACTICALLY GUARANTEED.

SO THIS IS WHAT YOU WERE UP TO, EH? CLEVER, ISSHIKI.

FWIP

HM, HM. WHAT'S THIS, NOW? "RULES AND REGULATIONS REGARDING SHOKUGEKI CHALLENGES ISSUED TO THE AZAMI ADMINISTRATION OVER THE DECLARATION OF THE DISBANDING OF SOCIETIES AND SEMINARS"...

SO BASICALLY THE MOP-UP WE'RE DOING RIGHT NOW. OKAY.

HENCEFORTH TO BE KNOWN AS THE ISSHIKI RULES.

TROMP

HE NAMED THEM AFTER HIMSELF? UGH. HOW ANNOYING.

~Rules and Regulations Regarding Shokugeki Challenges Issued to the Azami Administration Over the Declaration the Disbanding of Societies and Seminars

~Henceforth to be known as the Isshiki Rules~

Submitted by: Satoshi Isshiki

TROMP

SHOULD THE PARTY OF THE FIRST ISSUE A CHALLENGE, THE PARTY OF THE SECOND IS OBLIGATED TO ACCEPT.

TOTSUKI INSTITUTE RESEARCH SOCIETIES AND SEMINARS (HENCEFORTH REFERRED TO AS "THE PARTY OF THE FIRST") ARE PERMITTED TO CHALLENGE THE CENTRAL GOURMET ORGANIZATION (HENCEFORTH REFERRED TO AS "THE PARTY OF THE SECOND") TO A SHOKUGEKI IN REGARD TO REPEALING THE ORDER FOR THEIR DISBANDING.

FIRST ARTICLE (THE COMMENCEMENT OF THE SHOKUGEKI).

AND IT'S REALLY ANNOYING HOW HE'S USING WORDS LIKE "ARTICLE" AND "THE PARTY OF" TO MAKE THIS SOUND LIKE A LEGAL CONTRACT.

The Party of the Second

CENTRAL

Challenge!! ~Shokugeki~

Research Society

The Party of the First

#152 RECONNAISSANCE

...TO GET KICKED OFF THE COUNCIL.

EVERYONE? I HAVE SOMETHING TO SAY. BUT PLEASE TRY TO STAY CALM, OKAY?

I EXPECT SOMETIME WITHIN THE NEXT FEW DAYS...

BFFFFT

...I PLAN TO MAKE FULL USE OF MY POWER TO SET AS MANY THINGS IN ORDER AS POSSIBLE.

HOWEVER, WHILE I STILL HOLD MY SEAT ON THE COUNCIL OF TEN...

UNFORTUNATELY, I DON'T THINK THERE'S ANYTHING THAT CAN BE DONE ABOUT IT.

YOU WON'T BE THE SEVENTH SEAT ANYMORE?! NO! DON'T LET IT HAPPEN, SENPAI!

WHAT? WHY?!

Victory

LIKE WHAT?

KOFF KOFF

**A CLOSE-UP OF
THE CENTRAL BADGE**
IT'S THEME:
THE THISTLE, CALLED
AZAMI IN JAPANESE

FINE...

NO "BUTS" EITHER.

BUT...

DON'T "AWW" ME.

AWW, BUT THAT THING'S BIG AND CLUNKY! IT GETS IN THE WAY...

RINDO SENPAI, I DON'T SEE YOUR CENTRAL BADGE. PLEASE PUT IT ON.

CENTRAL

YOU ALL MAKE SURE YOU GOT YOUR BADGES ON TOO. UNLESS YOU WANT NENE TO YELL AT YOU.

AH, WELL. GUESS WE'D BETTER GET GOING.

DOOOM

EVEN NOW, THE FINEST WARRIORS CENTRAL HAS TO OFFER ARE OFF TO MEET THEM.

SUPERIOR OR INFERIOR MEANS LITTLE.

I THINK THEY SHOULD ALL JUST GIVE UP AND SAY I WIN.

I HAD THE MOST PROFITABLE BOOTH IN THE SLOPES FOR THE WHOLE MOON FESTIVAL.

UGH... WHY DO I HAVE TO ACCEPT CHALLENGES FROM A PACK OF INFERIORS?

C'MON, EIZAN! HOW LONG ARE YOU GONNA POUT BECAUSE YUKIHIRA BEAT YOU!

JUST CONSIDER IT ANOTHER PART OF YOUR STANDARD TRAINING.

ONE PUTS ONE'S BEST ON THE TABLE, NO MORE, NO LESS.

...

SWAT

I SEE THAT YOU HAVE NOT REMOVED YOUR DAUGHTER, ERINA NAKIRI, FROM THE COUNCIL.

I DOUBT ANY OF THEM WILL TAKE YOU UP ON IT THOUGH.

OF COURSE, IF YOU WISH TO RETURN TO THE COUNCIL, YOU COULD ALWAYS CHALLENGE ONE OF THE OTHER MEMBERS TO A SHOKUGEKI.

NO. OF COURSE NOT.

NOW THEN, ALLOW ME TO TAKE MY NEXT TURN AT THIS GAME, IF YOU WILL.

!

SOONER OR LATER, SHE WILL RETURN TO MY SIDE.

YES. AS PROMISED, WE HAVE GRACIOUSLY ACCEPTED THE CHALLENGES FROM THOSE SEMINARS AND SOCIETIES THAT PROTESTED THEIR ORDER TO DISBAND.

THE SHOKU-GEKI, SIR?

I AM CERTAIN THAT, EVENTUALLY, SHE WILL COME TO AGREE WITH ME.

THIS WAS SOMETHING WE'VE LONG SEEN COMING.

AND YOU SEEM LESS SURPRISED THAN *I* EXPECTED.

MY, MY. THIS WAS SOONER THAN I EXPECTED.

THE NOW-OPEN SEATS WILL BE FILLED AT A LATER DATE BY STUDENTS OF MY CHOOSING.

...AND THE THREE OF US WOULD NOT HAVE BEEN YOUR PREFERRED CHOICES FROM THE START. CORRECT?

HOWEVER, YOU ARE NOW DEAN...

...AND WHAT THEIR SEATS WILL BE. AFTER THE CANDIDATES ARE CHOSEN, THEIR FINAL RANKINGS ARE LEFT IN THE HANDS OF THE STUDENTS THEMSELVES THROUGH SHOKUGEKI.

EVERY YEAR, IT IS THE DEAN AND THE BOARD OF DIRECTORS WHO DECIDE UPON WHO WILL BE THE NEW CANDIDATES FOR THE COUNCIL OF TEN...

I AM GLAD YOU ARE SO UNDER-STANDING.

IN THE END, SHE WAS OUT-VOTED.

HOWEVER, THE OTHER MEMBERS ALL AGREED THAT HAVING ANYONE WHO DISAGREED WITH THE PRINCIPLES OF CENTRAL ON THE COUNCIL WOULD BE...*UN-PRODUCTIVE.*

I DON'T THINK THEY HAVE TO GET KICKED OFF THE COUNCIL!

C'MON! WHAT'S WRONG WITH THEM?!

RINDO KOBAYASHI DID PUT UP SOME RESISTANCE TO THE IDEA...

THIRD SEAT TOSUKE MEGISHIMA.

EIGHTH SEAT TERUNORI KUGA.

AND YOU, SEVENTH SEAT SATOSHI ISSHIKI.

MY THANKS FOR COMING ALL THIS WAY.

ALLOW ME TO GET STRAIGHT TO BUSINESS.

AS OF TODAY...

...ALL THREE OF YOU HAVE BEEN RELIEVED OF YOUR SEATS ON THE COUNCIL OF TEN MASTERS.

VRRRRM

KREEE

SEV-
ERAL
DAYS
LATER
...

WHAT ON EARTH IS GOING ON?!

ALL I KNOW...

DAD... AZAMI NAKAMURA... WHAT THE HECK HAPPENED BETWEEN YOU TWO?

HOW MUCH IS COINCIDENCE...

...AND HOW MUCH WAS PLANNED?

...IS THAT THE MAN NAMED JOICHIRO SAIBA...

...SITS SQUARELY IN THE CENTER OF THIS ENTIRE MESS!

...IS GETTING REVENGE.

NAKA-MURA. ALL YOU'RE DOING...

SALVATION? HA! I GUESS THAT'S ONE WAY TO SPIN IT.

WATCH. ALL OF YOU. THE STATE OF THE GAME BOARD IS ABOUT TO CHANGE... DRASTICALLY.

WE'RE LEAVING.

YES, SIR.

VRRRRRM

OH, HOW LUCKY I AM. I GET TO SHOW IT ALL TO SAIBA SENPAI'S OWN SON, AND IN PERSON!

BTAM

I'M SURE SENPAI WILL BE SO PROUD.

WHAT DID HE MEAN BY ALL THAT?

UM... I'M CONFUSED.

WELL, THEN. HOW MUCH IS COINCI-DENCE...

...AND HOW MUCH WAS PLANNED? THAT IS THE QUESTION.

CHUCKLE

SO THAT'S WHAT IT IS.

ANYWAY! WHAT I'M TRYING TO SAY IS THAT YOUR "REVOLUTION," OR WHATEVER YOU WANNA CALL IT, IS A ROYAL PAIN IN THE BUTT TO US.

WHAT'RE YOU MUTTERING ABOUT OVER THERE?

...?

...?

MY PLANS, THIS GRAND REVOLUTION THAT I HAVE BROUGHT TO TOTSUKI...

EVERY-THING!

SO WOULD YOU PLEASE STOP TRYING TO CHANGE THE SUBJECT?

OH, BUT I'M NOT. THIS IS ALL CONNECTED, SOMA YUKIHIRA.

AHAAA
...

I SEE.
YES, I
SEE NOW.

HUH?

HM?

...IN THE SAME GRADE AS SAIBA SENPAI'S SON?

...

I DIDN'T KNOW *YOU* HAD MET CHEF SAIBA, FATHER...

ME?

ERINA?

YOU KNOW OF SAIBA SENPAI?

HE'S MY DAD.

#151 THE WAR BEGINS

?!

"... "THE TRUE GAME IS ONLY JUST BEGINNING."

CAN YOU BELIEVE THAT CREEP AZAMI NAKIRI?! HE WAS ALL, LIKE...

WHAT A JERK!

RAAGH!

H-HUH?! W-WHAT?

C'MON, ERINA-CHI! YOU TOO! LET'S GO!

OH, NO, YOU DON'T. THAT'S A WASTE OF GOOD SALT.

YEAH! WE'RE NOT GONNA LET HIM COME INTO POLARIS EVER AGAIN!

WE NEED SALT! LET'S THROW SALT AND PURIFY ALL THE SPOTS HIS CREEPY FEET TOUCHED!

JOICHIRO SAIBA?

I NEVER KNEW YOU WERE FRIENDS WITH HIM, NAKAMURA SENPAI.

UMM... EXACTLY WHAT I SAID? HE'S MY DAD.

AND WHAT DO YOU MEAN BY THAT?

...

OH, THAT'S RIGHT. I GUESS IT'S NO SURPRISE PEOPLE OUTSIDE OF POLARIS DON'T KNOW.

THEY'RE JUST TWO PEOPLE WHO HAPPEN TO HAVE THE SAME NAME.

NO... NO, THAT'S IMPOSSIBLE.

HM? "SAIBA"? WHO IS SAIBA?

I SNAPPED ONE WHEN HE CAME TO VISIT BEFORE SUMMER VACATION.

HANG ON. I'VE GOT A PHOTO.

YUKIHIRA'S FATHER IS SOMEONE OF THAT CALIBER?

A FORMER SECOND SEAT?!

YUKIHIRA'S FATHER IS A MAN NAMED JOICHIRO SAIBA. HE'S A POLARIS ALUM AND FORMER SECOND SEAT ON THE COUNCIL OF TEN.

113

A RARE
SNAPSHOT
OF AZAMI
NAKIRI CAUGHT
COMPLETELY
OFF GUARD

108

PERSONALLY, I STILL THINK POLARIS IS A PRETTY COOL PLACE.

UH-HUH. I SEE. WELL, WHATEVER.

I MUST ADMIT, COMING HERE HAS TAKEN ME BACK A LITTLE.

AAH, THE DAYS OF POLARIS'S GOLDEN AGE, WHEN I LIVED HERE TOGETHER WITH SAIBA SENPAI...

COM-PLETELY UNLIKE THE STUDENTS HERE NOW.

HE WAS AN UNQUESTIONED GENIUS AND A SUPERLATIVE CHEF...

HUH?

HIS SKILL. HIS TASTE. EVERYTHING ABOUT HIM MADE IT ABUNDANTLY CLEAR THAT HE WAS BORN DIFFERENT, BORN GREATER THAN THE COMMON CHEF.

THOSE DAYS WITH HIM ARE THE MOST BELOVED DAYS OF MY YOUTH.

YOU MAY NOT KNOW THIS ALREADY, BUT...

UH, PARDON ME?

TP
TP
TP
TP
TP

NAKAMURA SENPAI.

YOU LIVED IN THIS DORM FOR YEARS, RIGHT?

AFTER ALL THAT TIME...

...DIDN'T YOU COME OUT OF IT WITH ANY FONDNESS OR ATTACHMENT TO THE PLACE?

MY, MY. WAS THAT AN ATTEMPT AT SCORN?

UNTIL MY GRAND REVOLUTION REACHES ITS FINALE...ITS *FINITION*...

...I WILL ALLOW HER TO HAVE HER SMALL FREEDOMS.

SCUZE ME, SIR.

I'VE JUST GOT A QUICK, DUMB QUESTION, IF YOU DON'T MIND.

COME ALL THIS WAY TO SEE ME OFF?

WHAT IS IT?

AAH. SOMA YUKIHIRA, WAS IT?

YES... BUT ARE YOU CERTAIN THIS IS WISE?

NO. I TOLD YOU THAT ALREADY.

I FAIL TO SEE THE PROBLEM WITH IT.

ARE YOU TRULY NOT BRINGING MISS ERINA BACK WITH YOU, SIR?

MY TRAINING HAS EMBEDDED ITS ROOTS TOO DEEPLY WITHIN HER FOR HER TO DO OTHER-WISE.

ERINA WILL RETURN TO ME.

...

...WILL RULE THE ENTIRE GAME BOARD.

THEN MY IDEAL, MY TRUE GOURMET...

NOW, THEN. I HAVE DONE WHAT I CAME TO DO, SO I WILL BE LEAVING.

I WILL SEE YOU LATER, ERINA.

WHRL

...?

IN FACT, THE TRUE GAME IS ONLY JUST BEGINNING.

...BUT YOU DO REALIZE THAT YOU AND THIS DORM ARE BY NO MEANS SAFE NOW, CORRECT?

BY THE WAY, A CELEBRATION OR TWO IS FINE...

...ARE MAKING STEADY ADVANCES ACROSS THE BATTLEFIELD THAT IS THE TOTSUKI INSTITUTE.

THE ELITE PIECES I HAVE PERSONALLY CHOSEN AND GATHERED TO MY CAUSE...

HOWEVER, CENTRAL REMAINS UNAFFECTED AND CONTINUES ITS EXPANSION.

TRUE, YOU DID DEFEAT EIZAN AND PROTECT YOUR DORMITORY FROM HIS MACHINATIONS.

IT IS ONLY A MATTER OF TIME BEFORE YOU FIND YOURSELF IN CHECKMATE.

ARE YOU TELLING ME...

THAT ASIDE, THERE IS ONE THING I CAN'T—WON'T—OVERLOOK.

...HE HAD ALREADY TAKEN THE THIRD SEAT ON THE COUNCIL AS HIS OWN.

AND BY THE TIME HE WAS OUR AGE...

HE'S A FORMER FIRST SEAT?!

IT SIMPLY HAPPENED TO BE AMONG THE GROUPS I WISHED TO SEE DISBANDED.

I DIDN'T ATTEMPT TO SHUT DOWN POLARIS SPECIFICALLY.

...WITH SHUTTING DOWN THE VERY DORM HE HIMSELF LIVED IN FOR YEARS?

...THAT THIS MAN WAS PERFECTLY FINE...

SHUDDER

AZAMI NAKAMURA

RISING THROUGH THE RANKS WITH UNPRECEDENTED SPEED, HE WON THE THIRD SEAT ON THE COUNCIL OF TEN IN THE FALL OF ONLY HIS FIRST YEAR IN HIGH SCHOOL.

BY HIS SECOND YEAR, HE HAD TAKEN THE FIRST SEAT.

THAT BY ITSELF WAS ENOUGH TO GUARANTEE HIM STARDOM IN THE HIGHEST CIRCLES OF THE CULINARY WORLD, BUT HE WASN'T SATISFIED. HE EVENTUALLY TURNED HIS EYES TO AN EVEN HIGHER RANK...

A PLACE WITHIN THE GASTRIC GODFATHER'S OWN FAMILY!

UNTIL SIR SENZAEMON BANISHED HIM FROM THE INSTITUTE AND STRUCK HIS NAME FROM THE FAMILY RECORDS.

GIVEN HIS SKILLS, HIS TRACK RECORD AND HIS STATUS, HE WAS A WORLD-CLASS CULINARY STAR WHO ALL BELIEVED WAS EMINENTLY WORTHY OF THE HONOR...

A HANDFUL OF YEARS AFTER HIS GRADUATION, HE MARRIED A LADY OF THE NAKIRI FAMILY AND WAS GIVEN THE NAKIRI NAME HIMSELF.

DON'T YOU THINK YOU'RE BEING AWFULLY COLD? ONE OF YOUR OLD STUDENTS HAS COME TO VISIT.

NOT ONLY THAT...

OH, COME, MISS FUMIO. YOU KNOW I GO BY *NAKIRI* NOW.

WHAT ?!

YAMMER

HE'S A POLARIS ALUM?!

SIR AZAMI, I TOOK THE LIBERTY OF DOING A LITTLE RESEARCH ON YOUR HISTORY.

APPARENTLY.

WAIT A MINUTE... HE'S AN INSTITUTE GRAD?!

EVERYONE, PLEASE CONTINUE TAKING GOOD CARE OF MY DAUGHTER.

...?!

YOU'RE NOT CAUSING THE RESIDENTS HERE ANY TROUBLE, ARE YOU?

YOUR REFINED UPBRINGING HAS LEFT YOU A LITTLE NAIVE ABOUT THE WAYS OF THE WORLD, I'M SURE.

IF SHE HAS DECIDED SHE WANTS TO STAY HERE, THEN SHE MAY DO SO.

I DO LIKE TO RESPECT ERINA'S DECISIONS.

I BELIEVE I SAID FROM THE OUTSET THAT MY PURPOSE HERE WAS JUST TO SPEAK WITH HER.

UM... SO YOU DIDN'T COME HERE TO TAKE HER BACK WITH YOU?

AND THE WHOLE INSTITUTE SAW YOU TRYIN' TO SHUT DOWN OUR DORM! NOW YOU STRUT IN HERE LIKE YOU OWN THE PLACE?!

L-LISTEN, WE KNOW EVERYTHING, YOU HEAR? WE HEARD ALL ABOUT THE NASTY AND CRUEL THINGS YOU DID TO ERINA-CHI!

F-FATHER?

...!

WSH

W-WHY ARE YOU HERE?!

STAY BACK! GET OUT!

COULD I ASK THAT YOU COME BACK AT ANOTHER TIME?

I'M AFRAID WE ARE IN THE MIDST OF A CELEBRATION RIGHT NOW.

I'M HERE TO SPEAK WITH ERINA.

DEAN, SIR. TO WHAT DO WE OWE THIS SURPRISE?

#150 GAMES

I JUST HAPPENED TO BE PASSING BY.

ERINA IS HERE, CORRECT?

#150 GAMES

HE'S HEADED STRAIGHT TO THE CAFETERIA?

PARDON ME.

!

SWFF

AND IF SHE IS?

*FOR MORE OF MISS ERINA'S BATTLES AGAINST THE MYSTERIOUS DEVICE KNOWN AS THE WASHING MACHINE, PLEASE SEE THE TITLE PAGE FOR CHAPTER 142 IN VOLUME 17.

KREEE

GYAAAH! P-P-PUT SOME CLOTHES ON!

WHAT ARE YOU DOING HIDING IN THE CORNER? COME OVER HERE AND JOIN US!

...

YOU'RE MAK-ING NO SENSE!

WHAT'S WRONG WITH WHAT I'M WEARING? YOU'LL GET USED TO IT SOON ENOUGH!

BING BONG

WHO WOULD COME BY AT THIS HOUR?

HUH? WAS THAT THE DOORBELL?

I'LL GET IT!

KREE

YES, WHO IS IT?

COME TO THINK OF IT, IT WAS A NIGHT LIKE THIS WHEN THE OLD DEAN DROPPED BY TOTALLY UNANNOUNCED...

TP TP TP

...IF THERE *IS* SOMEONE WHO CAN SAVE THE INSTITUTE FROM SIR AZAMI...

MAYBE, JUST MAYBE...

...IT'S HIM.

JOLT

FLEX

ARATO! NAKIRI!

THAT LOOK ON YOUR FACE WHEN WE HEARD OF YUKI-HIRA'S VICTORY...

!

IT WAS AS IF YOU ALSO SOMEHOW KNEW...

...THAT HE WOULD FIND A WAY.

YOU SEEMED QUITE ODD YOURSELF, HISAKO.

W-WHAT? ME? I-I DID?

WAH HA HA HA

YAMMER

YAMMER

ER! W-WELL... IT'S DIF-FICULT TO EXPLAIN...

WHATEVER MADE YOU BELIEVE SOMETHING LIKE THAT?

BUT I DO HAVE A... FEELING.

I HAVE NO REAL PROOF OF THIS...

RESISTING WON'T DO ANYTHING BUT GET THEM INTO MORE TROUBLE.

I JUST CAN'T COMPREHEND THIS.

EIZAN HAS ALL OF THE JUDGES IN HIS POCKET.

WAAAAAA

BACK WHEN THE DORMITORY WAS UNDER ATTACK...

...THAT YUKIHIRA WOULD WORK A MIRACLE.

...I SAW THE HOPE—NO, THE EXPECTATION...

BUT ON EVERY ONE OF THEIR FACES...

OH... THAT'S AMAZING.

WELL... YES. OF COURSE.

A WASHING MACHINE?

HISAKO, DO YOU KNOW HOW TO OPERATE A WASHING MACHINE?

MISS ERINA?

GLOOM

O-OH. OKAY.

...AND MANY VERY STRANGE THINGS--LOADS OF WHICH ARE RIGHT HERE IN THIS DORMITORY!

M-MY POINT IS THAT THERE ARE MANY NEW THINGS IN THE WORLD...

A-ANYWAY! FORGET ABOUT WASHING MACHINES FOR NOW!

*CULTURE-SHOCKED ERINA

AND THERE IN THE MIDDLE OF THEM...

...STANDS YUKIHIRA.

THEY TRULY ARE SUCH ODD PEOPLE.

SHEESH! WHAT IS GOING ON WITH THESE PEOPLE?!

WAH HA HA

...BUT EVEN THEY SEEM PERFECTLY ACCEPTING OF SOMEONE WEARING NOTHING BUT AN APRON!

I THOUGHT THE ALDINI TWINS WERE RELATIVELY NORMAL...

YOU HAVE THAT RIGHT, MISS ERINA! IN FACT, I WOULD EVEN GO SO FAR AS TO SAY THEY'RE OUTRIGHT STRANGE!

I KNEW IT. THE PEOPLE WHO LIVE HERE TRULY ARE ODD.

BLUSH

MISS ERINA?

THIS PLACE IS IMPORTANT TO ME TOO, Y'KNOW.

AWW... NO NEED TO THANK ME.

THANK YOU WITH ALL OF MY HEART. YOU SAVED OUR HOME.

THANK YOU, SOMA.

OH! I HEARD ALL ABOUT WHAT YOU DID TOO.

WELL, YEAH. OF COURSE.

ALL OF YOU DEFENDED THE DORM FROM EIZAN'S GANG OF ENFORCERS!

KINDA HARD NOT TO. I MEAN, WE HAVEN'T SEEN YOU AROUND HERE IN AGES.

SO YOU REALLY DIDN'T SELL US OUT, DID YOU?

MY, MY! YOU STILL DOUBT ME?

HEE HEE! YEAH. FOR ALL HIS GRUFFNESS, HE CARES A LOT ABOUT HIS FRIENDS.

...

H-HEY. QUIT IT.

Y'KNOW, YOU'RE A REAL GOOD GUY, IBUSAKI!

WE WEREN'T GONNA LET YUKIHIRA DO ALL THE FIGHTING BY HIMSELF.

OF COURSE, THE INSTITUTE IS STILL FIRMLY UNDER THE AZAMI ADMINISTRATION'S CONTROL.

ANYONE WHO MAKES SUCH A CHALLENGE WILL FACE VERY STEEP CONSEQUENCES IF THEY FAIL.

HOW-EVER...

WITH THIS, THE RIGGED-MATCHES PLAN THAT EIZAN HAD SPEARHEADED...

...HAS NOW BEEN COMPLETELY DERAILED!

YOU DID IT, SOMA!

YOU BROUGHT THE SHOKUGEKI SYSTEM BACK TO LIFE!

WHAT?! I WOULD NEVER!

YEAH. YOU NEVER KNOW WITH HIM. HE COULD HAVE DONE IT.

PSST PSST

TO BE HONEST, I WAS STARTING TO WONDER IF ISSHIKI SENPAI HAD SOLD US OUT.

WIPE

YOU SAID THE OTHER SOCIETIES HAVE BETTER CHANCES NOW. WHAT DID YOU MEAN BY THAT?

UM, I-ISSHIKI!

I THOUGHT ALL OF YOU UNDERSTOOD THAT ALREADY!

I LOVE THIS DORMITORY WITH ALL OF MY HEART!

O-OH, YES. ABOUT THAT...

IT HAS ALSO GUARANTEED THAT THE SHOKUGEKI WILL BE CONDUCTED FAIRLY AND WITH IMPARTIAL JUDGES!

...THE AZAMI ADMINISTRATION WILL ACCEPT ANY AND ALL SHOKUGEKI CHALLENGES IN RELATION TO THE ORDER TO DISBAND ALL SOCIETIES AND SEMINARS!

GOING FORWARD...

!

WITH THE OFFICIAL RESULTS OF TODAY'S SHOKU-GEKI...

...CENTRAL HAS ANNOUNCED A NEW POLICY.

A NEW POLICY?

ISSHIKI SENPAI!

WHERE THE HECK HAVE YOU BEEN?!

DO YOU HAVE ANY IDEA HOW ROUGH IT GOT AROUND HERE?!

I'M SORRY, EVERY-ONE.

NO MATTER HOW MUCH I WANTED TO HELP, I JUST WASN'T IN A POSITION WHERE I COULD DO ANYTHING.

...

...?

I AM STILL AN OFFICIAL MEMBER OF THE COUNCIL, AFTER ALL. EVEN A SMALL MOVE ON MY PART TO AID THE DORM...

...COULD HAVE BROUGHT EVEN MORE PRESSURE DOWN ON IT FROM THE AZAMI ADMIN-ISTRATION, AND YOUR SITUATION WAS ALREADY BAD ENOUGH AS IT WAS.

NOM

WHOA. SOMEBODY DOESN'T LOOK SATISFIED.

...I WANNA CHALLENGE HIM TO A REAL MATCH, WHERE WE'RE BOTH EVEN!

SOME-TIME SOON...

HEH. I KNOW EXACTLY WHAT YOU MEAN, YUKIHIRA.

RUMBL

BY THE WAY, THIS SHOKUGEKI LET US KEEP THE DORM OPEN, RIGHT?

THANKS TO YOU, SOMA, THEIR CHANCES ARE MUCH BETTER THAN THEY HAD BEEN.

SO WHAT ABOUT ALL THE OTHER SOCIETIES AND SEMINARS THAT WERE IN DANGER OF GETTING SHUT DOWN?

THOUGH NONE OF THEM ARE TRULY OUT OF THE WOODS YET, OF COURSE.

WHAT'S GONNA HAPPEN WITH THEM NOW, I WONDER?

BWAH?!

Polaris Foreve
Victory Part

YEAH! THAT MEANS YUKIHIRA'S ALREADY TOTALLY ON THEIR LEVEL, DOESN'T IT?!

HE CRUSHED *THE* NINTH SEAT OF THE COUNCIL OF TEN!

W-WELL, THAT'S ONE THING, BUT USING *CHAN* IS ANOTHER! THERE IS NO DIGNITY TO IT!

AWW! BUT YOU DON'T MIND WHEN YOSHINO CALLS YOU ERINA-CHI!

AND WHO ARE YOU CALLING NAKIRI-CHAN?!

EXCUSE ME?! YOU MUST BE KIDDING! DON'T BE SO RUDE.

YEAH! MAYBE HE COULD EVEN BEAT NAKIRI-CHAN TOO?

EIZAN SENPAI DIDN'T EVEN START THINKING ABOUT WHAT TO MAKE UNTIL HALFWAY THROUGH THE MATCH, AND HE STILL MADE A DISH THAT GOOD.

Y'KNOW... I WAS THE ONE WHO SET THE THEME.

GULP

...

SOMA?

149 HEAVEN AND HELL

YIKES! I'M SURPRISED YOU CAME OUT OF THAT ALIVE, MAN! SERIOUSLY!

SO Y'SEE...

BUT Y'KNOW? THINKING ON IT NOW, DOESN'T THAT MAKE IT ALL THE MORE AMAZING?

STILL, IT WAS TOUCH AND GO THE WHOLE WAY.

I FIGURED AS LONG AS I COULD GET THEM TO ACTUALLY TASTE MY COOKING, IT'D ALL WORK OUT IN THE END.

TAKUMI!

IF I HAD BEEN IN HIS SHOES, I WOULD HAVE DONE THE SAME.

HIS TERRITORY— HIS *HOME*— WAS THREATENED.

ER...GOOD EVENING TO YOU, ALDINI TWINS.

WOW. NOW *THIS* IS DIFFER-ENT.

BOW

WHOA! NAKIRI REALLY IS HERE IN THE DORM!

...HE'S CERTAINLY RELAXED.

FOR SOMEONE WHO JUST FINISHED AN INCREDIBLY STRESSFUL CONTEST...

C'MON IN AND EAT, GUYS!

ANYWAYS! TONIGHT'S A NIGHT FOR CELEBRA-TION!

TOTALLY RELAXED

ARTIST: YUTO TSUKUDA   RECIPE BY: YUKI MORISAKI

VOLUME 18
SPECIAL SUPPLEMENT!

YUKIHIRA-STYLE
STUFFED
CHICKEN WINGS!

INGREDIENTS
(SERVES 4/MAKES 16)

16 CHICKEN WINGS

150 GRAMS GROUND PORK

4 SLICES PORK JOWL

1/8 HEAD OF CABBAGE

1/2 BUNDLE OF LEEKS

2~3 SHIITAKE MUSHROOMS

2 THUMBS GINGER

2 CLOVES GARLIC

A 2 TABLESPOONS EACH SAKE, SOY SAUCE
1 TABLESPOON SUGAR

B 1 TABLESPOON EACH POTATO STARCH, SESAME OIL, SUGAR, SOY SAUCE
1 TEASPOON OYSTER SAUCE

SALT, PEPPER

60 GRAMS POWDERED CHEESE
100 CC WARM WATER
1 TABLESPOON VEGETABLE OIL

1 USE A PAIR OF KITCHEN SCISSORS TO REMOVE THE TWO BONES INSIDE EACH CHICKEN WING. MIX (A) TOGETHER, AND RUB THE DEBONED WINGS WITH IT.

2 DICE THE CABBAGE, LEEKS AND SHIITAKE MUSHROOMS. GRATE THE GINGER AND GARLIC. CHOP THE PORK JOWL INTO SMALL PIECES.

3 MIX THE GROUND PORK AND THE PORK JOWL TOGETHER IN A BOWL UNTIL THE MIXTURE LOOKS WHITISH. ADD (B) AND THOROUGHLY MIX TOGETHER THEN ADD IN THE CABBAGE, LEEKS, SHIITAKE MUSHROOMS, GARLIC AND GINGER, AND MIX AGAIN.

4 TAKE THE CHICKEN WINGS FROM (1), STUFF WITH 1/16TH OF THE MIXTURE FROM (3) AND PINCH CLOSED. REPEAT FOR ALL 16 WINGS.

5 HEAT THE VEGETABLE OIL IN A SKILLET OR A FRYING PAN. PLACE THE WINGS FROM (4) IN THE PAN SKIN-SIDE UP AND FRY UNTIL THE BOTTOMS ARE BROWNED. FLIP THEM OVER SKIN-SIDE DOWN AND DUST WITH POWDERED CHEESE. POUR IN THE WATER, COVER AND TURN DOWN TO LOW HEAT. LET STEAM FOR 10 MINUTES.

6 ONCE ALL THE WATER HAS STEAMED OFF AND THE WINGS ARE COOKED THROUGH, REMOVE FROM HEAT AND PLATE THEM BROWNED-SIDE UP. (DRIZZLE WITH SAUCE IF DESIRED. THEY CAN BE ESPECIALLY DELICIOUS AS A DONBURI RICE BOWL WHEN PUT ON TOP OF WHITE RICE AND DRIZZLED WITH SAUCE.)

● INGREDIENTS ●

2 TABLESPOONS EACH VINEGAR, SUGAR, KETCHUP
2 TEASPOONS EACH SOY SAUCE, CHICKEN BOUILLON
200 CC WATER
1 TABLESPOON POTATO STARCH
1 TEASPOON SESAME OIL

OPTIONS [MAKING THE SWEET & SOUR SAUCE]

1 PUT ALL THE INGREDIENTS INTO A POT, AND STIR TOGETHER WELL.

2 HEAT UNTIL BOILING. STIR THE MIXTURE UNTIL THICKENED.

SOMA.

WELCOME HOME.

THANKS!

YEAH! WE'VE GOT A PARTY TO START! A POLARIS-IS-SAVED PARTY!

OKAY, EVERYONE. I'M SURE WE ALL HAVE A LOT WE WANT TO TALK ABOUT. LET'S HEAD INSIDE.

OH! UM, THESE ARE FROM POLARIS'S GOLDEN AGE...

AND HELMETS?

WAIT. WHY IS EVERYTHING IN THE FRONT YARD SOAKED?

WELL, IT'S KINDA A LONG STORY...

AWESOME JOB, MAN!

STILL, HOW THE HECK DID YOU PULL OFF THAT WIN, YUKIHIRA?!

I STILL CAN'T BELIEVE YOU DID IT!

68

TROMP

TROMP

PTOO

DUN

....!

HA! TAKE THAT, YOU CREEPS!

YESSS! THEY'RE ALL LEAVING!

OH!

IT'S MY JOB TO MAKE SURE THE RIGHT PIECES ARE IN PLACE IN TIME.

THAT'S WHEN THE REAL FIGHT STARTS.

LOOKS LIKE IT ALL WENT DOWN JUST LIKE ISSHIKI SAID IT WOULD.

HUH! WELL, WELL.

POLARIS... STAYS.

THE EVICTION IS CANCELED.

....!

PULL OUT.

STARE

BLINK

TWITCH

...

FLUMP

EVEN...

...IF YOU SEND ANY OF THE TEN AFTER US.

...I WILL MAKE YOU PAY. UNDERSTAND?

JUST SO WE'RE CLEAR, IF YOU TRY ANY FUNNY BUSINESS WITH MY FRIENDS OR MY DORM MATES...

YOU MAY THINK WE'RE JUST SOME INFERIOR NOBODIES...

...BUT WE'RE NOT GONNA SIT HERE AND LET YOU STARE DOWN YOUR NOSES AT US.

YOU WANNA PICK A FIGHT WITH US? FINE.

WE'LL TAKE YOU UP ON IT, AND WE'LL GIVE YOU THE THRASHING OF YOUR LIVES!

HELLOOO, LADIES AND GENTLEMEN OF CENTRAL! YOU WATCHING?

W-WHAT ARE YOU—

HANG ON A SEC!

A-ALL RIGHT, EVERYONE! WE'RE PACKING UP AND LEAVING!

YOINK

I HOPE I DON'T STUTTER. THAT'D BE EMBARRASSING.

MAN. NOW THAT I THINK ABOUT IT, BEING ON TV IS REALLY KINDA NERVE-RACKING.

IF YOU'VE GOT SOMETHING TO SAY, MAKE IT QUICK!

AHEM

OH, RIGHT. OKAY.

THE REVOLUTION WAS COMPLETE! I EVEN MADE AN EXAMPLE OUT OF SOME FOOL! IT WAS SUPPOSED TO HAVE WORKED!

NO. IMPOSSIBLE. THIS CAN'T BE HAPPENING!

...AND THREW A WRENCH INTO THE WORKS!

BUT THEN YUKIHIRA CAME ALONG...

RRRGH!

SWFF

D-DO NOT GET A BIG HEAD, BOY!

DOES THAT MEAN I GET HIS SPOT AS THE NEW NINTH?

I DID JUST BEAT THE COUNCIL'S NINTH SEAT IN A SHOKUGEKI...

HANG ON A SEC.

WHAT?!
H-
HOW?!

HOW THE HECK DID HE MANAGE TO PULL IT OFF?!

HOLY CRAP! I CAN'T BELIEVE IT!

B W A A A H ?!

!

W A A A A A

Y-Y-YU-E-I-RA!

YOU'VE GOTTA BE KIDDING ME! IS THIS EVEN REAL?!

...

POLARIS

YUKI-HIRA!

#148 TRIUMPHANT
RETURN

Soma Yukihira 3-0 Etsuyo Eizan

MARUI! WHAT'S WRONG?! WHAT HAPPENED?!

DMP
DMP

SOMA...

SO...

...THIS MEANS POLARIS DORMITORY DOESN'T GET SHUT DOWN, RIGHT?

KRAAASH

IT SOUNDS LIKE THEY BUSTED THROUGH THE WESTERN BARRICADE!

POLARIS

CRAP! DID YOU HEAR THAT?!

WAIT.

SOMETHING ISN'T RIGHT.

DASH

DANG IT! I KNEW WE'D ONLY BE ABLE TO HOLD OUT FOR SO LONG...

51

REINDEER MEGUMI

AS SEEN IN THE ILLUSTRATION AT THE FRONT OF THIS CHAPTER CELEBRATING THE THIRD ANNIVERSARY OF *FOOD WARS!*

OOH! THIS IS SO WARM AND COMFY!

HEY,
EIZAN
SENPAI.

SWFF

47

IT'LL SMASH YOUR FOSSILIZED LITTLE WORLD TO PIECES.

GO ON. DIG IN.

NGH...

GULP

SIZZ

SIZZ

WHOA, WHOA! YOU AREN'T GONNA—

OI!

SWFF

44

I HAVE DONE COUNTLESS TASTINGS FOR INNUMERABLE CLIENTS...

...BUT HARDLY A ONE OF THEM HAS EVER DARED CONTRADICT ME.

AFTER ALL, MY SENSE OF TASTE WAS ALWAYS UNEQUIVOCALLY CORRECT.

YES, I SEE, MISS ERINA.

WE SHALL DO WHATEVER YOU SUGGEST.

HOW SHALL WE REVISE THE RECIPE?

...LEADING TO ANSWERS THAT NO ONE COULD HAVE PREDICTED.

BUT HERE AT POLARIS, CRAZY IDEA AFTER CRAZY IDEA BOUNCE OFF ONE ANOTHER...

...WHO AREN'T EVEN WORTH GIVING THE TIME OF DAY TO.

TO YOU ALL, I'M SURE WE'VE GOT TO SEEM LIKE A BUNCH OF NOBODIES...

WHAT'S THAT ORGANIZATION YOU ALL WORK FOR NOW? CENTRAL SOMETHING OR OTHER?

WAAAAAA

...IS SOMETHING THAT MY DORM MATES AND I CAME UP WITH WHEN WE WERE EXPERIMENTING.

THE IDEA OF USING TOMATOES FOR SOMETHING LIKE THIS...

HOW DID YOU EVER REACH THIS IDEA?!

...?

POLARIS

I WILL ALLOW NO ONE TO BARGE IN HERE AND TREAT YOU WITH DISRESPECT!

DON'T YOU WORRY, MISS ERINA!

HISAKO.

I FIND THEM... ODD.

THE PEOPLE WHO LIVE IN THIS DORMITORY.

YES?

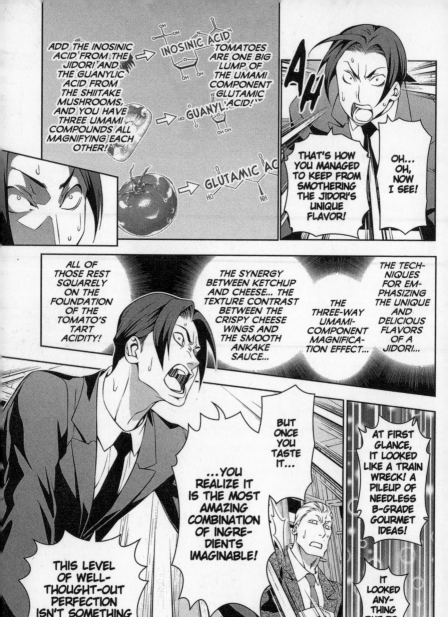

ADD THE INOSINIC ACID FROM THE JIDORI AND THE GUANYLIC ACID FROM THE SHIITAKE MUSHROOMS, AND YOU HAVE THREE UMAMI COMPOUNDS ALL MAGNIFYING EACH OTHER!

INOSINIC ACID

TOMATOES ARE ONE BIG LUMP OF THE UMAMI COMPONENT GLUTAMIC ACID!

GUANYLIC ACID

GLUTAMIC AC

AH

THAT'S HOW YOU MANAGED TO KEEP FROM SMOTHERING THE JIDORI'S UNIQUE FLAVOR!

OH... OH, NOW I SEE!

ALL OF THOSE REST SQUARELY ON THE FOUNDATION OF THE TOMATO'S TART ACIDITY!

THE SYNERGY BETWEEN KETCHUP AND CHEESE... THE TEXTURE CONTRAST BETWEEN THE CRISPY CHEESE WINGS AND THE SMOOTH ANKAKE SAUCE...

THE THREE-WAY UMAMI-COMPONENT MAGNIFICA-TION EFFECT...

THE TECH-NIQUES FOR EM-PHASIZING THE UNIQUE AND DELICIOUS FLAVORS OF A JIDORI...

BUT ONCE YOU TASTE IT...

AT FIRST GLANCE, IT LOOKED LIKE A TRAIN WRECK! A PILEUP OF NEEDLESS B-GRADE GOURMET IDEAS!

...YOU REALIZE IT IS THE MOST AMAZING COMBINATION OF INGRE-DIENTS IMAGINABLE!

THIS LEVEL OF WELL-THOUGHT-OUT PERFECTION ISN'T SOMETHING THAT CAN BE HIT ON OUT OF THE BLUE!

IT LOOKED ANY-THING BUT RE-FINED!

KETCHUP
?!

IT'S
KETCHUP.

...INTO
A SPECIAL
HOUSE-BLEND
SWEET 'N'
SOUR SAUCE!

I USED
GOOD OL'
TOMATO
KETCHUP TO
MAKE THAT
ANKAKE
SAUCE...

JOLT

IT'S
PERFECT FOR
ALLEVIATING THE
THICK OILINESS
OF SOME DISHES,
GIVING THEM
A FRESH AND
TANGY FLAVOR.

IT'S
ESPECIALLY
HANDY FOR
CHINESE
COOKING, WHICH
COMMONLY
MAKES USE OF A
VARIETY OF OILS.

SWEET 'N' SOUR SAUCE IS
USED IN A LOT OF DISHES,
FROM OBVIOUS ONES LIKE
SWEET 'N' SOUR PORK, TO
REGIONAL VARIETIES OF
TENSHINHAN CRAB OMELET
OVER RICE, AND EVEN
SEAFOOD DISHES LIKE
DEEP-FRIED COD!

AND TO TOP
IT ALL OFF,
PARMESAN
CHEESE AND
TOMATOES
ARE A GREAT
MATCH FOR
EACH OTHER!

THE BASE BROTH
OF THE SAUCE IS
FROM A STOCK
I MADE FROM
THE JIDORI'S
CARCASS, SO OF
COURSE IT WILL
PAIR WELL WITH
THE WING
MEAT.

NOT ONLY
THAT, IT ALSO
BRINGS OUT
THE SATSUMA
JIDORI'S
RENOWNED
DELICATE
AFTERTASTE!

...IT WIPES OUT
THE CLOYING
GREASINESS
OF BOTH THE
PARMESAN CHEESE
AND THE PORK
JOWL, LEAVING
ONLY THEIR RICH
FLAVORS BEHIND.

SO BY
ADDING THE
TART ACIDITY
OF TOMATO-
BASED KETCHUP
TO MY ANKAKE
SAUCE...

SOMA YUKIHIRA, THIS IS GOOD! LIKE, REAL GOOD!

WHOA!

YOU WOULD THINK BY ADDING POWERFULLY FLAVORED INGREDIENTS LIKE CHEESE AND PORK JOWL THAT THE OVERALL TASTE WOULD BECOME HEAVY AND CLOYING, BUT THAT ISN'T THE CASE AT ALL!

EVEN THE DELICATE AFTERTASTE UNIQUE TO THE SATSUMA JIDORI HAS BEEN VIVIDLY ENHANCED!

AND UNDER THOSE LIES THE TENDER AND SPRINGY CHICKEN MEAT THAT FLOODS THE MOUTH WITH ITS UMAMI-LADEN JUICES WITH EACH BITE!

THE CRISPY CRUNCH OF THE SAVORY PARMESAN WINGS. THE THICK AND SMOOTH ANKAKE SAUCE.

GRIN

WHAT THE HECK IS THAT INGREDIENT? TELL ME! NOW!

YUKIHIRA, QUIT STALL-ING!

I SEASONED THAT JIDORI STOCK WITH ONE SPECIAL SECRET IN-GREDIENT.

THE ANSWER TO THAT IS IN THE ANKAKE SAUCE.

WHAT?! WHY?! HOW?!

AFTER ALL THOSE UNTHINKABLE THINGS YOU DUMPED INTO THIS, HOW IS THE JIDORI'S FLAVOR STILL SO STRONG?!

I'M GONNA TUCK RIGHT IN!

OOOH! YES! FINALLY! GIMME GIMME!

ORDER UP! HERE YA GO.

RINDO KOBAYASHI, YOU AREN'T REALLY GOING TO—

WELL, DUH. OF COURSE I AM! DIDN'T YOU SEE HOW MUCH EIZAN LOVED IT?

AFTER THAT, THERE'S NO WAY I'M NOT GONNA TRY IT FOR MY-SELF.

....!

REINDEER ERINA

AS SEEN IN THE ILLUSTRATION AT THE FRONT OF THIS CHAPTER CELEBRATING THE THIRD ANNIVERSARY OF *FOOD WARS!*

#147 BEGIN THE COUNTERATTACK!

EIZAN'S TOP FUNNY FACES

ARBITRARILY 1ST PLACE
(AS OF CH. 146)

23

ONE BITE... JUST ONE BITE CAN'T HURT. RIGHT? WE CAN JUDGE AFTER.

W-WAIT.

?

UMM...

SKWEEZ

THERE'S NO POINT IN TASTING THIS SLOP. I WON'T DO IT!

WHAT ON EARTH ARE YOU SUGGESTING?

W-WELL, WE ALREADY KNOW WHICH WAY WE'RE VOTING! WHERE'S THE HARM?

WHAT ?!

PSST
PSST

IF YOU WILL, THEN I GUESS I MIGHT TOO...

....!

O-OH, UM... I'M SORRY, BUT I THINK I WILL.

?!

SIZZ TUNK SIZZ

HERE YA GO.

IMPOSSIBLE! SIMPLY IMPOSSIBLE!

...WHY NOT GIVE IT A QUICK TASTE TO SETTLE THINGS FOR SURE?

C'MON, NOW. IF YOU'RE THAT CONVINCED...

RIDICULOUS!

...

GLANCE

WH

ENOUGH OF THIS! IT'S TIME TO PASS JUDGMENT AND—

TAP

I ALREADY TOLD YOU, I DON'T NEED TO TASTE IT TO KNOW HOW BAD IT IS!

FLINCH

HM? WHAT IS IT?

GULP

SOMETHING WRONG, EIZAN SENPAI?

QUIVER

QUIVER

QUIVER

QUIVER

?!

WHAT?!

DIDJA MAYBE THINK, JUST FOR A SECOND...

...THAT MY STUFFED WINGS WERE REALLY GOOD?

...!

WHAT COULD POSSIBLY BE GOOD ABOUT THAT B-GRADE TRIPE?!

YOU WERE NEVER, EVER...

...FIT FOR THE TOTSUKI INSTITUTE IN THE FIRST PLACE.

THIS JUST PROVES IT.

DLOOP

CHEW

CHEW

CHEW

CHEW

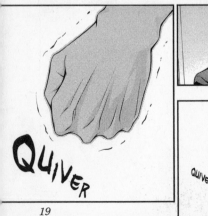

HM?

QUIVER

QUIVER

19

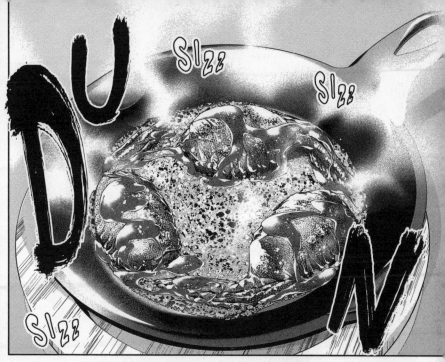

DU
DOW
N

SIZZ

SIZZ

SIZZ

SIZZ

I BET YOU MADE THIS WHOLE THING UP AS YOU WENT ALONG, JUST DUMPING IN WHAT-EVER.

STK

SIZZ

WHAT'S THE POINT OF THAT ANKAKE SAUCE?

PAH! WHAT CRAP.

18

PLOOSH

WZAPOK

HE'S GOING FOR THE STOCK!

PLISH

SIZZZZ

THIS HERE IS THE LAST STEP, I PROMISE.

I'VE ADDED SOME POTATO STARCH TO THE STOCK I MADE FROM THE JIDORI'S BONES TO THICKEN IT INTO A SAUCE.

WISH WISH WISH WISH WISH WISH

SIZZZZZZ

KRAKL

SIZZZZZ

POP POP POP POP POP KRAKL POP POP

NOW!

THE WATER HAS COMPLETELY STEAMED OFF.

POP KRAKL

THERE.

MAYBE, BUT...

WE OUGHT TO PASS OUR JUDGMENT RIGHT NOW AND BE DONE WITH THIS SHAM.

HOW MANY TIMES MUST I SAY THIS IS A ALL A WASTE?

OI! HOW ABOUT YOU SAY SOMETHING, YUKIHIRA!

CEASE THIS FRUIT-LESS STRUG-GLE AND GIVE UP!

SHH!

IS THERE SOMETHING MORE WE'RE MISSING?

HE STILL HASN'T ADDED THAT CHICKEN STOCK.

SIZZZZ

14

THERE. SEE? I TOLD YOU.

WITH EVERY STEP...

...IT'S BECOMING MORE AND MORE CLEAR THAT THIS TRAVESTY OF A DISH IS NOTHING MORE THAN A POOR ATTEMPT AT B-GRADE GOURMET.

HEH HEH...

HA HA HA HA!

HIS DISH IS THE POLAR OPPOSITE OF YOUNG EIZAN'S REFINED AND ELEGANTLY SIMPLISTIC MASTERPIECE!

HE HAD ALREADY DESTROYED THE UNIQUE FLAVORS OF THE JIDORI THE MOMENT HE ADDED PORK JOWL TO THE FILLING.

HE IS DOING NOTHING BUT SMOTHERING THE SATSUMA JIDORI'S RENOWNED DELICATE FLAVOR WITH IDEA AFTER GAUDY AND UNNECESSARY IDEA!

BUT NOW HE'S GOING TO SLATHER IT WITH CHEESE TOO?

13

EVEN WHEN FRYING POT STICKERS INSTEAD OF BOILING THEM, WATER IS ADDED.

STEAMING THE INNER FILLING IS AN IMPORTANT PART OF COOKING THE POT STICKERS.

TIME TO ADD THE LIQUID.

AND BY USING WARM WATER INSTEAD OF COLD, THE OUTER SHELL IS LESS LIKELY TO BECOME STICKY.

IT SEEMS YUKIHIRA IS WELL AWARE OF THAT...

...AS HE'S ADDING PIPING HOT WATER TO THE SKILLET.

GRIN

WIP

SH

SPSHUU

IF YOU HAVE ANY PREP WORK YOU NEED TO DO, GET ON IT.

I THINK I'LL USE THE KITCHEN HERE AND DO JUST THAT.

OH YEAH, THERE WAS SOMETHING HE STARTED BEFORE THE MATCH BEGAN. GUESS IT WAS THAT STOCK.

S I Z Z

WHAT ARE THOSE FOR?

CHICKEN STOCK AND POT STICKERS? WHAT THE HECK IS HE TRYING TO DO?

THERE! LOOKS LIKE THE SKILLET IS HOT ENOUGH NOW.

THEN THERE'RE THOSE JARS HE'S HOLDING.

GOOD. LOOKS LIKE THE CHICKEN SKIN IS CRISPING NICELY.

GENERALLY ON THE SMALL SIDE, A SKILLET IS PERFECT FOR COOKING UP SINGLE-PERSON PORTIONS OF A DISH.

ONCE HOT, IT STAYS HOT, MAKING IT IDEAL FOR SEARING AND FOR HEATING INGREDIENTS EVENLY.

THE SKILLET— MADE OF CAST IRON, THIS THICK, HEAVY PAN CAN BE HEATED UP TO VERY HIGH TEMPERA-TURES.

MY, MY! YOUNG EIZAN IS SO CONSIDERATE TO GO ALONG WITH THIS FARCE.

IT ISN'T AS IF WE CAN'T ALREADY TELL HOW POOR THAT CLUELESS BOY'S DISH IS GOING TO BE.

SO GO ON! HAVE FUN MAKING THE LAST DISH YOU'LL EVER COOK AT TOTSUKI!!

BUT IT'S GONNA BE THE LAST THING YOU EVER DO!

ALL RIGHT...

GRIND

YOU WANNA GO? LET'S DO IT. SHOW ME WHAT YOU GOT.

HERE WE. GO.

?

OH, RIGHT! ALMOST FORGOT. I'D BETTER GO GET THAT!

DMPA

DMPA

...

CHICKEN STOCK MADE FROM THE JIDORI'S BONES?

WHAT'S THAT?

8

18

Table of Contents

MEGUMI TADOKORO First Year High School

Coming to the big city from the countryside, Megumi made it into the Totsuki Institute at the very bottom of the rankings. Partnered with Soma in their first class, the two became friends. However, he has a tendency to inadvertently yank her around from time to time.

ALICE NAKIRI First Year High School

Erina's cousin, she has spent much of her life overseas with her parents learning cooking from a scientific perspective through molecular gastronomy.

RYO KUROKIBA First Year High School

Alice's aide, he specializes in powerful, savory seafood dishes. His personality changes drastically when he puts on his bandanna.

HISAKO ARATO First Year High School

Erina's exceptionally loyal and devoted aide, she is skilled in medicinal cooking. Her current worry is the proliferation of her nickname, Secretary Girl.

ETSUYA EIZAN Second Year High School

Ninth seat on Totsuki's Council of Ten. He is a naturally talented chef, and his work as a consultant gives him connections throughout the industry.

RINDO KOBAYASHI Third Year High School

The current second seat on Totsuki's Council of Ten, Rindo is friendly, sociable and easygoing. She met Soma during the Moon Festival and finds him intriguing.

AZAMI NAKIRI

Erina's father, he imposed an unspeakably harsh training regimen on his daughter in her youth. It was so bad Senzaemon banished him from the institute.

CHARACTERS

SOMA YUKIHIRA First Year High School

Helping out at his family's restaurant since he was little, Soma trained as a chef with the goal of someday surpassing his father. Out of junior high, he's suddenly sent off to culinary school. He's skilled, but sometimes invents questionable new recipes.

Shokugeki no SOMA

ERINA NAKIRI First Year High School

Granddaughter of Senzaemon Nakiri, dean of the Totsuki Institute, she has a sense of taste so refined, famous restaurants across the nation come to her to taste test their dishes. She is a member of Totsuki's Council of Ten Masters, the institute's highest decision-making student body.

STORY

Soma grew up helping to cook at his family's restaurant, Yukihira. But one day his father enrolls him in Japan's premier culinary school, the Totsuki Institute. Having met other students as skilled as he is and with similar goals, Soma has grown a little as a chef.

The first major act of the Azami administration is to disband all clubs and societies at Totsuki! Polaris Dorm also gets caught in the crosshairs, and the ninth seat, Eizan, is there to personally deliver the order for everyone's eviction! The student body resists these changes, and many clubs challenge Central to a shokugeki. But Eizan stacks the deck against the challengers by bribing the judges! Seeing the hope fade in his friends' eyes, Soma steps up and challenges Eizan to...a shokugeki?!

Food Wars!
SHOKUGEKI NO SOMA

Volume 18
Shonen Jump Advanced Manga Edition
Story by Yuto Tsukuda, Art by Shun Saeki
Contributor Yuki Morisaki

Translation: Adrienne Beck
Touch-Up Art & Lettering: Mara Coman
Design: Alice Lewis
Editor: Jennifer LeBlanc

SHOKUGEKI NO SOMA © 2012 by Yuto Tsukuda, Shun Saeki
All rights reserved.
First published in Japan in 2012 by SHUEISHA Inc., Tokyo.
English translation rights arranged by SHUEISHA Inc.

The stories, characters and incidents mentioned in this publication
are entirely fictional.

Printed in the U.S.A.

Published by VIZ Media, LLC
P.O. Box 77010
San Francisco, CA 94107

10 9 8 7 6 5 4 3 2 1
First printing, June 2017

www.viz.com

THE WORLD'S MOST
CUTTING-EDGE MANGA

SHONEN JUMP
ADVANCED
www.shonenjump.com

RATED
T+
FOR OLDER TEEN

PARENTAL ADVISORY
FOOD WARS! is rated T+ for Older Teen and is
recommended for ages 16 and up. This volume
contains sexual situations/humor.
ratings.viz.com

Yuto Tsukuda

This year's resolution—
wake up while it's still
technically morning.

Shun Saeki

My wife took this picture.
Isn't it amazing?!
It's really awesome!
Like, really!

JUN 2 1 2017

About the authors

Yuto Tsukuda won the 34th Jump Juniketsu Newcomers' Manga Award for his one-shot story *Kiba ni Naru*. He made his *Weekly Shonen Jump* debut in 2010 with the series *Shonen Shikku*. His follow-up series, *Food Wars!: Shokugeki no Soma*, is his first English-language release.

Shun Saeki made his *Jump NEXT!* debut in 2011 with the one-shot story *Kimi to Watashi no Renai Soudan*. *Food Wars!: Shokugeki no Soma* is his first *Shonen Jump* series.